The
Lauder Light Railway

by
Andrew M. Hajducki
and
Alan Simpson

THE OAKWOOD PRESS

British Library Cataloguing in Publication Data
A Record for this book is available from the British Library
ISBN 0 85361 495 4

Typeset by Oakwood Graphics.
Repro by Ford Graphics, Ringwood, Hants.
Printed by The Witney Press, Witney, Oxon.

**To the children of Lauderdale, that they may know something
of Maggie Lauder and her ilk.**

Lauder in the 1950s with the Eagle Hotel prominent and an interesting collection of British cars of the period. The message on the back of the card, sent to 'Betty' in Yorkshire, reads: 'We have had some rain. I don't like it a bit but it just suits your dad. I shall be glad to get back. There is nothing here. I shall not come again. Mum'. *Authors' Collection*

Title page: The seal of the Lauder Light Railway Company. *Glasgow Museum of Transport*

Published by
The Oakwood Press
P.O. Box 122, Headington, Oxford OX3 8LU

Contents

Lauderdale looking towards Collie Law and Oxton - the railway ran from left to right in the middle distance. *A.M. Hajducki*

Lauder Town Hall, June 1914. This photograph was taken by W.F. Jackson, the General Manager of the North British Railway, and shows the 18th century municipal building which formerly housed the local gaol and the splendid gas lamp and drinking trough with cast-iron cattle feet - the lamp, unfortunately, did not survive a collision with an errant lady motorist's car in the 1920s.   *Glasgow University*

Introduction

The Lauder Light Railway was one of the many rural lines promoted under the auspices of the Light Railways Act 1896 - an enlightened, if ultimately doomed, attempt to open up the more remote areas of Britain in the era when the motor car was in its infancy and the signs were clear that the Railway Age was coming to an end. Opened only a few months after the end of Queen Victoria's long reign, the diminutive trains on this virtually unknown by-way made their way laboriously up and down the gradients between Fountainhall, Oxton and Lauder for barely 30 years before the passenger service succumbed to bus competition, while the remaining goods service dwindled away to a mere skeleton before being finally laid to rest in the month which saw the inauguration of the first transatlantic jet service.

The beautiful hill country of Lauderdale is now, once again, remote from the railway and yet its quaint little branch line lingers on in fond local memory and folklore. The remains of the line are slowly vanishing and to those to whom Lauder is just one more of the historic Border towns and villages which slow traffic up on the spectacular A68 high road to Edinburgh, few will now be aware, or even care, that once upon a time farmers and schoolchildren, sheep and potatoes, could travel in the wee train pulled by 'Maggie Lauder' as she puffed her way up and down through the rolling green hills and quiet valleys. The authors can but hope that this book will keep her memory alive.

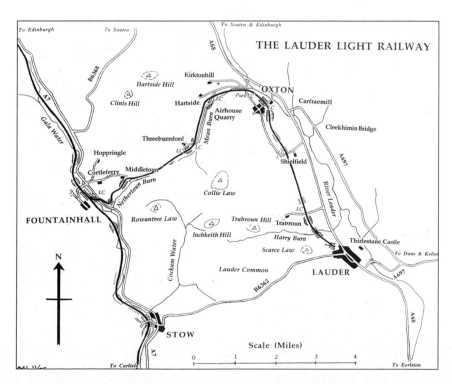

5

Thirlestane Castle, Lauder. This view of the ancestral home of the Lauderdales was taken by W.F. Jackson in 1914 and, somewhat unusually for his photographs, does not show Snark the dog!
Glasgow University

Oxton village - this pre-war view of this small settlement shows the Tower Hotel built for the opening of the railway.
Authors' Collection

TOWER HOTEL AND MAIN STREET, OXTON

B 9988

Chapter One

Genesis
THE COMING OF THE RAILWAY

'Of ilka place it is the wale, The sweet and pleasant Lauderdale'
Old Rhyme

The parishes of Lauder and Channelkirk lie at the north-western tip of Berwickshire and comprise the rich valley known as Upper Lauderdale and the bare and windswept hills which surround it. Through the parishes runs the great high road to Edinburgh, 25 miles away, and which nowadays, as the A68, carries the business and holiday traffic from Northumberland and the Borders into the lowlands of Scotland. This road passes out of the county at Soutra, 1,100 feet above sea level, and at a point marked by the famed snow gates which bear witness to the bleak, wild winter weather often found there.

Flowing southwards through Lauderdale, long known both for its associations with the Border ballads and its beautiful scenery, is a small tributary of the Tweed called the Leader Water, which rises in the Lammermuir Hills and flows down past Carfraemill towards Lauder, a small and ancient town with a long history and the centre of the large and scattered parish of the same name. The remainder of the population of Upper Lauderdale is to be found in hill farms and dale hamlets while the only other settlement of any size at all is the small village of Oxton, some five miles to the north of Lauder and situated in Channelkirk parish.

The area was first settled in prehistoric times and traces of this period can be found in a number of hillforts, hut circles and standing stones which still can be seen, together with flints and arrowheads which have on occasions been turned up by the spade and plough. At a later date the Romans and their highway, Dere Street, passed through the valley and when Christianity reached Berwickshire, the monks of Melrose built their own road called the Girthgate through Lauderdale in order to gain easier access to Soutra Aisle and Edinburgh. It is said that, as a boy, Saint Cuthbert, while tending sheep on the banks of the Leader, had his great vision of angels conducting the soul of St Aidan to heaven. Cuthbert was referred to by Bede as 'the child of God' - a fact which may have been reflected in the early name of the parish of Channelkirk - 'Childerchirke'. By mediaeval times Lauder was establishing itself as an important local centre and focus for much of the surrounding lands and the town had the distinction of being granted a charter of novodamus by James IV in 1502 to make it a Royal Burgh, the only one in Berwickshire.

The subsequent history of Lauderdale was a tumultuous one with many unwelcome (but sometimes arguably justified) incursions from the South. But it was a domestic incident which made it become notorious. This occurred when, in 1482, King James III was encamped in the vicinity of the burgh and on his way to deal with the English and attempt to recover the town of Berwick-upon-Tweed for the Scots. Several of the Scottish nobles met in the old kirk of Lauder and formed a plot which resulted in Archibald, Earl of Angus, or 'Bell the Cat' as he became better known, being responsible for hanging six of the King's minions from the bridge over the Leader Water. At a later stage family feuds led in 1598 to the destruction of the Lauder Tolbooth and murder was the culmination of the power struggle between local families including the Lauders and the Maitlands, the latter having their seat at Thirlestane Castle just outside the town. A century and a half later Prince Charles Edward Stuart stayed at Thirlestane Castle on his way to invade England and Sir John Cope was said to have lodged in the town while fleeing from the Battle of Prestonpans in 1746.

By the middle of the 19th century the population of Lauder was just over two thousand, divided almost equally between the burgh and the parish and in common with many other areas of rural Scotland the number of inhabitants was undergoing a slow and inexorable decline. The habits and character of the people of Lauder was summed up by the Reverend Peter Cosens, the parish minister, in the following terms,

> It may be affirmed of the people, on the whole, that they enjoy, in a reasonable degree, the comforts and advantages of society, and that they are contented with their situation; as one indication of which it may be stated that few families in the parish, - not more than four or five, - have in recent times, emigrated from the land of their fathers. Their character is, no doubt, as in every other place, considerably diversified, some being neither wise nor good; but in general they are well informed, - orderly in their conduct, - and observant of the ordinances of religion. Poaching, though instances of it may be occasionally detected, is not prevalent; and smuggling does not seem to exist.

There were no industries in the area apart from agriculture and in the words of the 1895 *Ordnance Gazeteer of Scotland,*

> Some little trade with the surrounding country districts is carried on, but the commercial importance of Lauder is of the slightest description. It maintains its communication with the world at large chiefly in virtue of being a convenient centre for trout-fishers . . . Though Lauder contains some neat and well-built houses, and has its suburbs adorned with a few neat villas, it presents on the whole a neat and dull aspect.

The town did, however, have one adornment without which a Victorian burgh would not have been complete - a gas works which was opened in 1842.*

Oxton, or Ugston as it was also called, was a village of some 200 inhabitants, situated a mile to the east of the ancient parish church of Channelkirk. There was little industry here but a vibrant local economy based on agriculture. The village possessed a number of flourishing local organisations including a parochial library, a total abstinence society, a friendly or burial society and the Oxton Bovial Society, a splendid example of 19th century self-help which on payment of an average annual fee of four shillings provided help towards the purchase of a new cow in the event of a member's beast dying. The population of Channelkirk parish, although in slight decline, was more stable than that of Lauder parish largely due to the fact that local farms were still attracting

---

* The gas works were situated at Burn Mill and were of the single retort type, costing £800 to construct. They outlived the railway, being finally closed in 1965 by which time they were said to have been 'of considerable antiquarian interest' even though the gas supplied apparently left much to be desired in terms of cleanliness and pressure. Electricity reached the area in 1932 thanks to the Scottish Southern Electricity Supply Company.

labourers; in the latter half of the century the number of people living in the parish hovered at around the 600 mark, in contrast to the present total of just over half of this amount. There was, however, some discontent and in the words of the *New Statistical Account of Scotland* of 1833:

> What this parish chiefly wants to promote improvement, to encourage industry and to contribute to the comfort of the labouring-classes, is the residence of land owners. Almost all the land belongs to absentees, who seldom or never see their property here and, consequently, never think of making any alterations either for ornamenting or improving it.

The principal activity of Lauderdale was, as it is now, agriculture and on the higher ground black-faced sheep were kept and their wool was an important source of revenue to the hill-farmers. In lower lying areas cross-bred sheep and cattle competed for space with potatoes, turnips, some corn and other arable crops. In all fairness, although Upper Lauderdale was and is a reasonably fertile area, even more so after the agricultural improvements of the latter half of the 18th century, it was never so profitable to the farmer as the richer lands of East Lothian or the Merse* and local farms in consequence remained large in size and relatively undeveloped.

Lauder itself was a self-contained burgh and had its own corporation which sat in the distinctive little Town House and administered local affairs† while a large number of inns and public houses catered for both the passing traffic and local needs. An unusual system of land-holding which gave rights to the Common and to the Burgess Acres (and which still survives today) gave the burgh a unique distinction and the townsfolk jealously guarded their property rights. The nearest markets to Lauder were at Kelso, 17 miles away to the south-east and Dalkeith, 16 miles to the north and reached by the recently improved turnpike road over Soutra. According to the *New Statistical Account*

> Very ample means of communication are enjoyed by the parish. It has a post-office in the town, and a daily mail, brought by the curricle which runs through Lauderdale between Edinburgh and London . . . On [its] roads travel five public carriages, which pass through Lauderdale, and four of them through Lauder, every lawful day to and from Edinburgh, Dunse, Kelso, Newcastle, &c. The two principal bridges cross the Leader, the one in the upper part of the parish, and the other a little to the east of Lauder. These, as well as the smaller bridges and the fences, are kept in good condition.

The age of the stagecoach in Berwickshire was, however, almost at an end and by 1845 two major railway schemes had been authorised, one being the new main line from Edinburgh to Berwick and the south, which passed through the eastern part of the county. The other was the Edinburgh & Hawick Railway which was to pass down the valley of the Gala Water in neighbouring Midlothian and which was to have stations at Fountainhall and Stow, both some five miles or so across the ridge of hills which divided the counties to the west of Upper Lauderdale. The fore-runner of the Edinburgh & Hawick scheme was an ambitious plan for a 'Midland' trunk route from England to Scotland, first proposed in 1843. Leaving the existing Newcastle & Carlisle Railway at

---

* An ancient name for the alluvial plain of the River Tweed
† Lauder remained a self-governing entity until the local government reorganisation of 1975; since April 1996 it has been part of the new Scottish Borders unitary authority.

Gilsland (about mid-way between Hexham and Carlisle) this line was to run northwards to Newcastleton where it would then have taken the way of the later Waverley Route to Edinburgh. This scheme came to naught but the northern half was resurrected as the Edinburgh & Hawick whose Bill received Royal Assent on 31st July, 1845; work began on the line shortly thereafter.

During the course of construction of the Edinburgh & Hawick an incident, long remembered thereafter locally, occurred. A shopkeeper from Lauder had travelled to Galashiels, some 10 miles to the south, in order to sell his goods there and when he refused to sell items to the navvies engaged on the railway construction works there, on the not altogether unreasonable premise that they were unlikely to pay him for the same, a near riot ensued. The unfortunate shopkeeper was then pursued back to his native town by an enraged mob and was only saved from disaster when a detachment of Dragoons were sent up from Piershill Barracks in Edinburgh and eventually managed to restore order.

The Edinburgh & Hawick was opened to all traffic as far as St Boswells in November 1849 under the auspices of the North British Railway (NBR), which was already on its way to becoming the largest railway company in Scotland. Already the benefits of connection to the growing railway network were becoming apparent to communities throughout Scotland and it was for these reasons that the inhabitants of Lauderdale began to turn their thoughts towards securing a railway of their own. In 1846, as part of the great railway mania that swept Britain, a line to be called the Berwickshire Central Railway had been promoted to run from a junction with the Edinburgh & Hawick line at a point south of Heriot to Oxton and Lauder, over the same route as was eventually followed by the Lauder Light Railway half a century later. From Lauder it would have extended southwards to Earlston before swinging to the east and passing through Smailholm before terminating at Kelso where it was to join a projected North British branch line from Tweedmouth. Plans for the Berwickshire Central were deposited with the Board of Trade in London but little more was heard of the scheme. Thereafter, Kelso was served by the NBR branch, which was opened in June 1850 from St Boswells, and by the North Eastern Railway which had been extended from Tweedmouth to make an end-on junction and included the only two stations in Scotland to be owned by an English railway company - Carham and Sprouston.

After the failure of the Berwickshire Central scheme local agitation for a railway continued and in April 1852 a public meeting was held in Lauder at which it was proposed to construct a branch line from Fountainhall, where it was to form the junction with the Edinburgh & Hawick line, to Oxton and Lauder along the same route as the previously proposed route for the Berwickshire Central. At that meeting, which was chaired by the Chief Magistrate of the Burgh, a Mr Valance, 24 gentlemen, with a Mr Broomfield as secretary, were appointed as a provisional committee. In October of that year these gentlemen issued a Prospectus in which it was stated that the required capital for the line would be £40,000 and the approximate annual revenue was stated as being £5,450. The Engineer appointed was Charles Japp of Edinburgh, a well-known figure in North British circles, and it appears that a preliminary survey of the route was carried out. Despite the fact that prospective shareholders were given a qualified promise of a 6 per cent annual dividend, the careful farmers of Lauderdale were not tempted by the scheme and to quote an early account, 'promotion, persuasion and percentage were all in vain.'

By 1863 a branch line owned by the independent Berwickshire Railway but worked from its inception by the North British had reached Earlston, some six miles to the south of Lauder, from the county town of Duns and two years later the line was extended to St Boswells, where it joined at Ravenswood Junction the Edinburgh & Hawick line - the latter was within a short time to become better known as the Waverley Route from Carlisle and the south to Edinburgh via the Border towns. It does, however, seems curious that at this time no attempt had been made to link Lauder with Earlston along the valley of the Leader as this would have been a relatively short and easily graded line which would have connected Lauder more directly to its main agricultural markets in the Borders. But given the depressed state of the financial markets in the 1860s it was perhaps thought such a project would not have been economically attractive.

The next proposal for a railway to Lauder was a revival of the previous plan for a branch line from Fountainhall and it was stated, somewhat optimistically, that the scheme would provide Lauder with 'direct railway communication with the metropolis' when in October 1870 a public meeting was held in the town presided over by Mr William Dickinson of Longcroft. At this meeting a report which had been prepared by the firm of Macnay and Nimmo, engineers, was adopted with great enthusiasm and unanimity. Within six months the sum of £2,800 had been raised by public subscription and the Lauder Town Council promised a further £2,000. Eventually a total of £31,000 had been pledged to this project but, following a survey of the proposed route, enthusiasm is said to have declined and for reasons which are not altogether clear the project was quietly abandoned.

The project for a railway to Lauder was revived in 1883 when Messrs Meik and Sons, engineers of Edinburgh, offered to survey alternative routes from Stow to Lauder and Ormiston to Lauder. For some years a horse-drawn bus service had been operated by a private contractor, Thomas Henderson, from Lauder to Stow over the four miles or so of hill-road across the Common; because this service was designed to connect with certain trains at Stow the North British had paid a subsidy to the contractor to ensure that the service was kept running.* The promoters of the railway estimated that in the year 1882-3 a total of 6,450 passengers had used the Lauder to Stow bus service and it was therefore proposed that powers be sought to build a line from Fountainhall (four miles north of Stow) and which would bridge the Edinburgh to Galashiels turnpike road and then run via Middletoun to a station on the main road at Carfraemill, close to Oxton village. From here the line would run alongside the road from Soutra to a terminus at Lauder. Again the scheme came to naught.

Towards the end of the decade, there was a certain amount of agitation for a

---

* The timekeeping of this service was said to verge on the erratic and the last part of the run down the steep hill to Stow village and station was often completed at an alarming speed. On one occasion Mr Henderson, on seeing the tell-tale plume of smoke in the distance, was said to have asked his passenger, the parish minister of Lauder, if he believed in the power of prayer 'because otherwise we're going to miss the train' - one suspects that the power of prayer might have been necessary (or at least advisable) to ensure a safe arrival at the station, whether or not the connection was made.

series of new lines to be constructed throughout the area, as it was felt that the railway monopoly held by the North British was generally working against the interests of the manufacturers and the inhabitants of the Border counties, in particular those of Hawick whose Town Council enthusiastically supported such schemes.   This agitation culminated in proposals for a 'New Border Railway' network to be worked (or perhaps built and worked) by the Caledonian Railway, the great rival of the NBR. The New Border system was to consist of a main line from Berwick to Lockerbie, by Hawick and Galashiels and a secondary line from Edinburgh to Pencaitland, Humbie, Lauder, Kelso and Mindrum, with a branch from Lauder to Galashiels. Quite how the fearsome gradients which would have been involved in a line which would have had to cross the flank of the Lammermuirs would have been surmounted by steam power was not apparent, but serious consideration was given locally to these proposals and in a letter to the local press from 'X.Y.', an inhabitant of Lauder, it was said that,

> This matter must commend itself not only to the inhabitants of Hawick, but it also ought to receive the hearty support and co-operation of Galashiels, Lauder &c. Those towns, especially the latter, will be benefitted to an extent which, at the first glance, can scarcely be realised by the adoption of the proposed route from Edinburgh . . . via Lauder . . . The latter route would open up an entirely new district which, offering so many attractions to the farmer, the sportsman, the tourist, &c. only awaits railway communication to make it one of the most popular and prosperous in Scotland. It appears to me that if the commissioners of Lauder, Galashiels, &c., were thoroughly alive to the interests of the towns they represent, they should at once co-operate with Hawick and cordially invite the Caledonian Company to enter the field. The first question that naturally would arise would be, will it pay? To this I should unhesitatingly answer, Yes.

Not surprisingly the proposed Border Railway scheme was too much to expect even the ambitious Caledonian Railway, ever willing to cock a snoot at its main rival, to embark upon and the North British monopoly was to remain unchallenged.

Here the matter might have rested had it not been for the advent of the Light Railways Act 1896. This legislation was passed in an attempt to open up new areas by means of railways which were built to a lighter specification than normal, and with relaxed operating requirements which permitted considerable savings and costs without adversely affecting safety. Provision was made for local and national government subsidies in appropriate cases. Prior to this in order to construct a railway for public traffic across lands belonging to others a great deal of money had to be spent on promoting a Bill through Parliament to secure the necessary powers to build the line, even though there was no guarantee that such a Bill would overcome the inevitable opposition and become an Act. The effect of the 1896 legislation, although already several years too late, was to enable such lines to be constructed and worked with a minimum of expense. The mechanism adopted was for the promoters of such a line to secure a Light Railway Order under which a line could be authorised by the Light Railway Commission, a statutory body set up under the Act. Experience of light railways had been gained by the study of continental lines and tramways but ironically it was the proposal for a road to be constructed between Oxton and Fountainhall that led to the successful promotion of a railway to Lauder.

In December 1895 a large meeting was held in the schoolroom at Oxton to hear a report from the sub-committee appointed to formulate a petition from the inhabitants of upper Lauderdale to the District Committee of the Berwickshire County Council on the subject of a road from Oxton to Fountainhall. The report stated that the local agitation for such a road had once again revived the idea and the sub-committee, having waited for over a year to know the results of that movement, and being unable to negotiate any advantageous terms with the North British Railway Company for a road or a railway presented their petition to the District Committee. The District Committee in turn did not feel that the general lack of local support for a road would warrant the building of such a road. The two proposed road schemes were to cost £1,610 and £3,358 apiece and it is perhaps curious that in view of this fairly low expenditure no road was in fact ever built between Oxton and Fountainhall - even today it is necessary to make a lengthy detour via Lauder Common or Soutra in order to travel on a public road westwards from Oxton.

The meeting went on to pass a vote of thanks to the sub-committee and was then addressed by Dr Gibb, of Boon , who spoke on the subject of light railways and he was said to have given a racy, full, and graphic account of the various modes suggested for meeting the wants of the district - by light railways, steam tramways, and auto-motors. He said that his own preference was for a light railway and a statistical analysis had shown that such a railway would yield a satisfactory return and he suggested that action should be taken as soon as the government was ready to pass the Light Railways Bill. A parish standing committee was then appointed to consider the matter. At a contemporaneous meeting of the Eastern District Committee of the Berwickshire County Council the subject of a light railway to Oxton and Lauder was discussed and resolutions were passed:

1. That light railways, under an improved system of procedure, are advantageous, and that the Lauderdale district is in a position to benefit therefrom in an especial degree;
2. That state aid and local enterprise are desirable, and essential to the introduction of a light railway in that district;
3. That the committee do not consider themselves qualified to say anything as to the construction of such a railway, further than that the gauge should be the same as that of the other railways authorised by the state.

What is perhaps interesting is that the local newspapers devoted much space at this time to the phenomenon of the Horseless Carriage and it was stated that:

The subject of horseless carriages is one of such importance to the people of the Borders that we make no apology for again referring to it. It is hoped by some that the vehicle to which Mr. J.C. Macdona, MP, referred to in the House of Commons recently, has a big future ahead of it. It is the invention of M. Daimler, and won the recent race of horseless carriages between Paris and Bordeaux. It is in appearance a sort of four-wheeled phaeton . . . Another invention is an electrical horse which could run for ten hours without refreshment, and take its next meal in ten minutes. By this invention the need of light railways was entirely done away with. Every farmer could have his own produce wagon and take it along the roads at the highest speed allowed by the authorities , at a cost of fourpence per hour per horseload . . . it is pretty certain that part of the legislative work of next session will be the repeal of the ridiculous law which prohibits any automatic carriage to run in the streets at a rate exceeding four miles an hour, and requires that it should be proceeded by a man waving a danger signal in the shape of a red flag . . . At present the signs point to petroleum as the power to be employed, electricity not having yet reached the stage of development when it is either the cheapest or the most convenient motor.

and a subsequent article in the *Berwickshire Advertiser* entitled 'Horseless Carriages versus Light Railways' concluded that the motor car might be a suitable alternative to the light railway in the country districts of Berwickshire. But despite this prescience of the shape of things to come it was the railway and not the motor car which was the first to conquer Lauderdale.

The horse bus which connected Lauder and Stow before the coming of the railway.
Public Record Office

Chapter Two

A Mighty Change
THE BUILDING OF THE LINE

'Cheer up, my lads, a mighty change,
Has swept across our dale
The old stage coach has yielded thus,
To carriage, steam and rail.'
'The Lauder Light Railway'

With the passing of the Light Railway Act in 1896 the mechanism was set up which would enable Lauder to receive its railway. Consequently, at the Berwickshire County Council meeting of 15th December, 1896 the Chairman of the Council laid before it 'a formal notice to owners of land and others' which had been received from the solicitors for the promoters of an order to authorise the making of a light railway from Fountainhall station to Lauder. It was said that nobody knew who the promoters of this line were but their solicitors, Messrs Millar, Robson & Maclean, Writers to the Signet, Edinburgh required affected landowners to state any objection to property being taken for the purpose of the proposed railway line. Members then discussed the issue and it was said that although the proposed railway had the approval of the whole Lauder district neither the North British Railway Company nor any member of the council could shed any light on who the promoters were, but it was suggested that the promoter was 'an engineer with a capitalist who has money lying.'

It soon became apparent that the application had been made by the two major local landowners, William Montagu Hay, the Tenth Marquis of Tweeddale (the Chairman of the North British, who had his seat at Yester House in Gifford) and Frederick Henry Maitland, the Thirteenth Earl of Lauderdale (proprietor of the Thirlestane estate just outside the town of Lauder) and that the proposed name of the concern was to be 'The Lauder Light Railway'. An application was made to Berwickshire County Council for the grant of a sum not exceeding £15,000. The capital of the proposed company was to be £45,000 made up of 4,500 shares of £10 each and the cost of constructing the line was estimated at £48,308 13s. In the words of a contemporary report in the *Berwickshire Advertiser,*

Estimates we know, are generally exceeded, and the promoters of the company have wisely, we think, provided for power to borrow £15,000 more. It appears that of the capital, the North British Railway Company are to subscribe £15,000, and undertake the working of the line, provided that the County Council of Berwickshire and the Burgh of Lauder subscribe other £15,000. It seems singular that the railway should not be carried on a little further, and joined to the Berwickshire line at Greenlaw, Gordon or Earlston. The promoters of the undertaking, no doubt, have good reasons for stopping at Lauder, but we hope some day that the railway will continue in the direction we indicated, and then across to Coldstream, where it could join the Berwick and Kelso line. The object is one that may be commended to the consideration of the owners of property, and the inhabitants in the district. Meanwhile, some difference of opinion seems to exist as to the desirability of starting the Lauderdale Light Railway at Fountainhall, and the people of Dalkeith are agitating to have it begun at that town. They contend that the line would be profitable if commenced at Dalkeith as the district that would be served by it would contribute more traffic in the shape of agricultural produce and minerals than would be got starting the railway from Fountainhall. It is also stated that the journey from Lauder to Dalkeith via Fountainhall would take 91 minutes, and the fare would be 2s 1½d., while the direct route from Lauder to Dalkeith, which is 19½ miles by road, might be less by railway, would take an hour and a quarter, and the fare would be 1s. 8d. These are points which, we have no doubt, the promoters of the undertaking will take into consideration before they finally decide which route to adopt.

This latter scheme was still considered to be viable and according to the *Dalkeith Advertiser,*

The Berwickshire County Council have approved of the Lauder-Fountainhall Scheme, but that was to be expected, as £45,000 had been guaranteed for that purpose. But that does not knock that alternative scheme on the head as might be supposed. A light railway could be made as far as Soutra, and would be a great service, or, as has been suggested, it could be made to go in an easterly direction to Humbie and Upper Keith. Now that a large and representative committee has been appointed, the scheme should not be allowed to fall through.

A number of public meetings took place in Dalkeith and Lauder and there appears to have been much public support (although little in the way of financial support!) for a line which would have been 20 miles long and very expensive both to build and operate. It seemed to be acknowledged that the Dalkeith line would be an alternative to the Fountainhall scheme and enthusiasts of the scheme stated that it would open up a rich agricultural area with mineral resources and, most important of all, a land with great potential for tourists. The latter claim was somewhat odd given the fact that the area was one of pleasant although unspectacular moorland countryside and that the only real tourism consisted of walkers and fishermen, neither of which would have sustained a railway of such magnitude.

The route of the original line was to be as follows. Starting at Fountainhall station on the Waverley Route, the line was to swing east, bridging the Gala Water before crossing, on the level, the main Edinburgh-Hawick road. Close to Burnhouse the line was then to climb in a north-easterly direction up to a summit between Middletoun and Threeburnford, before descending towards Oxton and then travelling southwards through the dale and across land which was held in common by the town to a terminus just outside of Lauder. The previous estimate of the cost of building the line was confirmed by Messrs Cunningham, Blyth and Wishart, Engineers, and was made up as follows: earthworks £14,623 2s. 6d., bridges - public roads £500, stream works £1,500, culverts and drains £2,000, metalling of roads and level crossings £367, permanent way including fencing £15,408 13s. (i.e. £1,480 per mile), permanent way for sidings and cost of junctions £1,000, stations £2,000, contingencies £3,889 17s. 6d. and land and buildings, 80 acres, £5,520. The share capital was to be £45,000 of which sum the North British Railway was empowered to subscribe £30,000.

The draft Light Railway Order was then prepared and it seemed that the long expected project of a railway from Fountainhall to Lauder would soon be an accomplished fact. On 10th April, 1897 the *Border Record* printed the following report:

On Saturday in the Town Hall, Stow, a public enquiry regarding the proposed Light Railway from Fountainhall to Lauder was held by the Light Railway Commissioners, the members present being the Earl of Jersey and Colonel Boughey, and the Commissioners' secretary, Mr Bert Ince. There was a large attendance of persons interested from Lauder, and from the proposed Gala Water end of the proposed line.

Mr F.T. Cooper, advocate, Edinburgh, was the counsel for the promoters of the line, Mr David Dundas, advocate, Edinburgh, counsel for the Gala Water District Committee of the Mid-Lothian County Council, Messrs J. & F. Anderson, WS*, for Mr Borthwick of Crookston, Messrs Lindsey, Howe & Co, WS for the Baroness Reay of Stow.

Mr Cooper opened the case for the promoters by stating the ends they sought by the line - improved communication of the Lauder District with the North British Railway system at Fountainhall. Briefly expressed, he said, the three objectors' opposition to the proposal was, that the promoters made no provision for fencing or accommodation works, that by a proposed level-crossing over, and its proximity to, the public road shortly after leaving Fountainhall Station, the safety of the public was in danger; and that about the same point in the line of route the railway would interfere with the amenity of Burnhouse. With regard to the level-crossing, and the general averment of danger to the public, he submitted that such crossings were contemplated by the Light Railways Act, and what he objected to was that the promoters should be compelled to put up expensive screenings and bridges which might be of absolutely no use whatever.

Mr Benjamin Blyth, consulting engineer to the NB Railway Company, said a bridge over the Gala Water Turnpike and fencing the line of railway from end to end would add considerably to the expense. With regard to the amenity of Burnhouse, he did not think any portion of the line would be visible from the house. Under cross-examination of Mr Dundas, witness said that the Gala Water Road, over which it was proposed to carry the line on a level-crossing, was a highway between Edinburgh and Carlisle, but with trains running at 15 miles an hour he did not think there would be any serious risk to the moderate amount of traffic on the turnpike. A bridge at that place might cost about £1,000.

Mr George Rankin, WS, Lauder, said the local feeling there and in the district was in favour of the railway. He stated the inconvenience they suffered from conveyance of passengers and merchandise over a bad road to Stow. The laying of a line had long been wished for, but efforts to construct it had been defeated in not being able to raise the money. Lauder Town Council and the West District Committee of the Berwickshire County Council, as well as the Council itself, were in favour of the scheme, and the Council had asked power to advance money to carry it out. The West District Committee apprehended no danger in respect to level-crossings and made no objection to them. The larger part of the line lay in Berwickshire. In addition to the favourable feeling in Lauder, the feeling in the four parishes particularly interested (Lauder, Channelkirk, Legerwood and Westruther) was also unanimous in favour of it. In answer to a question from Mr Dundas, witness said he came there at the request of the Lauder Town Council and the West District Committee of the Berwickshire County Council.

In the other evidence led by Mr Cooper for the promoters, Provost Moore, Lauder, corroborated Mr Rankin's evidence. The population of Lauder Parish, he said, was 1,600, and of Channelkirk 550. Of the four parishes named only two of these would benefit directly from the railway. Dr R. Shirra Gibb, farmer, Boon, stated the Upper Lauderdale was unanimous for the proposed line. It would be of immense value for the agricultural interest of the locality. At present they have to drive cattle and sheep, and to cart to and from the railway a great distance. That morning he had passed ten carts on the road from Stow Station to Lauder - seven laden with coal and three with merchandise. Mr Robert

* WS: Writers to the Signet are and were members of an ancient and exclusive society of solicitors in Edinburgh which is, happily, still with us.

LAUDER LIGHT RAILWAY ORDER, 1898.

ORDER

MADE BY THE

LIGHT RAILWAY COMMISSIONERS,

AND MODIFIED AND CONFIRMED BY THE

BOARD OF TRADE,

AUTHORISING THE CONSTRUCTION OF A

LIGHT RAILWAY BETWEEN FOUNTAINHALL RAILWAY STATION AND LAUDER, IN THE COUNTIES OF MIDLOTHIAN AND BERWICK.

Presented to both Houses of Parliament by Command of Her Majesty.

LONDON:

PRINTED FOR HER MAJESTY'S STATIONERY OFFICE,
By DARLING & SON, LTD., 1–3, GREAT ST. THOMAS APOSTLE, E.C.

And to be purchased, either directly or through any Bookseller, from
EYRE & SPOTTISWOODE, EAST HARDING STREET, FLEET STREET, E.C., and
32, ABINGDON STREET, WESTMINSTER, S.W.; or
JOHN MENZIES & Co., 12, HANOVER STREET, EDINBURGH, and
90, WEST NILE STREET, GLASGOW; or
HODGES, FIGGIS, & Co., LIMITED, 104, GRAFTON STREET, DUBLIN.

1898.

Light Railway Order for the Lauder Light Railway, 1898.

Dickinson, farmer, Longcroft, corroborated Dr Gibb's evidence.

Evidence was led for the objectors, of which the following were the principal points: Mr A.W. Belfrage (of Messrs Belfrage & Carfrae, consulting engineers, Edinburgh) considered the plans on behalf of the County Council of Mid-Lothian, as affecting the public interest. In his opinion the level-crossing at Fountainhall would be dangerous, and he thought it was absolutely the duty of the Council to object. The proper way to provide the railway at this point, he considered, would be to divert the road and have a bridge. With regard to the proposed bridge over Gala, he thought it should be of four spans of 25 feet each, instead of one of 50 feet. Mr Moffat (of Messrs J. & F. Anderson) and Mr John R Lumsden, farmer, Fountainhall, gave evidence bearing on the flooding of the haugh land on the Gala side. Mr T.Y. Ramsay, road surveyor, Gorebridge, gave evidence with regard to the traffic on the public road, and the alleged danger through the proposed level-crossing, and the proximity to said road at this point.

Mr David Pringle of Torquhan, convenor of the Gala Water District Committee of the Mid-Lothian County Council, gave it as his opinion that the part of the proposed line in dispute, shown in the plan, constituted a grave danger to the public, and an inconvenience and danger to traffic generally. Owing to the sharp turn and the steep gradient, it might not be possible to draw trains up in time to prevent accidents; and unless some protection was afforded the order should not be passed. A most feasible plan was that proposed by Mr Belfrage to divert the road and carry the railway over it; and if, as had been stated, the railway was going to be such an advantage to Lauder, and also profitable to the shareholders, it was perfectly reasonable to ask that this provision should be made. If the level-crossing were granted, without gates, sheep passing along the road would be certain to stray on the line.

The enquiry was adjourned and the Commissioners visited the Fountainhall end of the proposed railway.

A lengthy wait then followed. At the end of the year anxious letters began to appear in the local press asking why nothing appeared to have happened and criticising the local elected representatives for their apparent lack of interest in the proposed railway. The criticism, however, should have been directed more against the Board of Trade in London rather than any other party for without their sanction nothing could progress. Eventually the wheels of officialdom turned and on 30th June, 1898 'An Order made by the Light Railway Commissioners and modified and confirmed by the Board of Trade authorising the construction of a Light Railway between Fountainhall Railway Station and Lauder in the Counties of Midlothian and Berwick' was passed. The Order provided for the setting up of an incorporated body known as the Lauder Light Railway Company authorised to build a standard gauge line '10 miles 1 furlong or thereabouts in length' along the agreed route, the works therefore to be completed within five years. Among specific provisions were 'a bridge over the Gala Water with a single span of not less than fifty feet', certain gated level crossings and cattle grids (described as 'cattle-guards or other suitable contrivances . . . as to prevent cattle or horses passing along the road from entering upon the railway') at ungated crossings. Three clauses in the Order were of particular importance:

The Company shall not use upon the railway any engine carriage or truck bringing a greater weight than twelve tons upon the rails by any one pair of wheels.

The company shall not run any train or engine upon the railway at a rate of speed

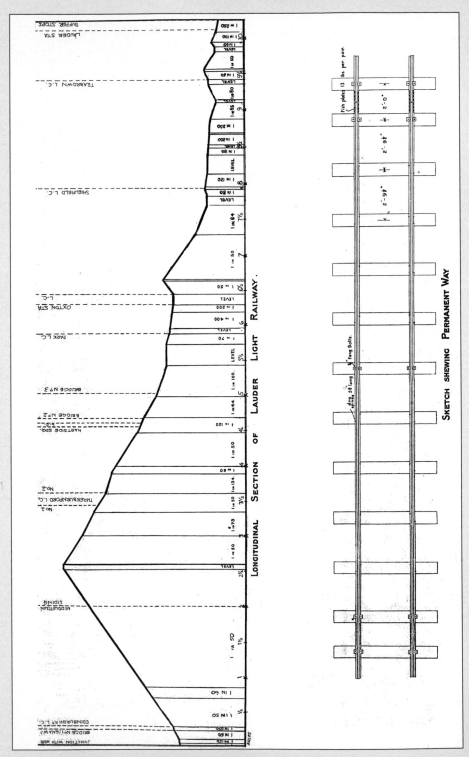

LONGITUDINAL SECTION OF LAUDER LIGHT RAILWAY.

SKETCH SHEWING PERMANENT WAY

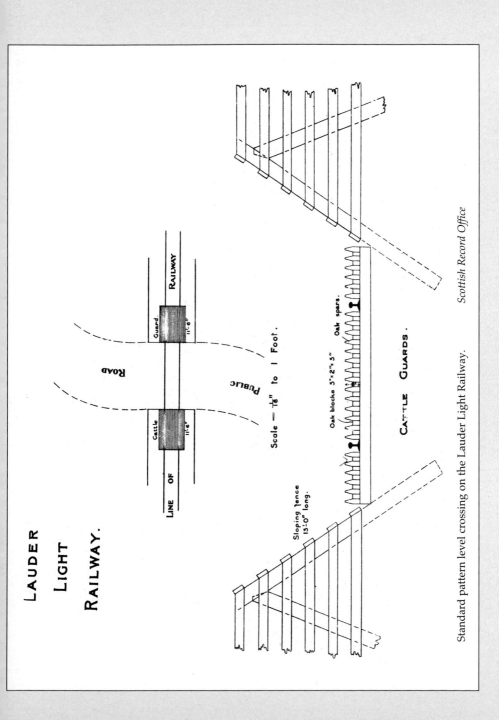

Standard pattern level crossing on the Lauder Light Railway.

Scottish Record Office

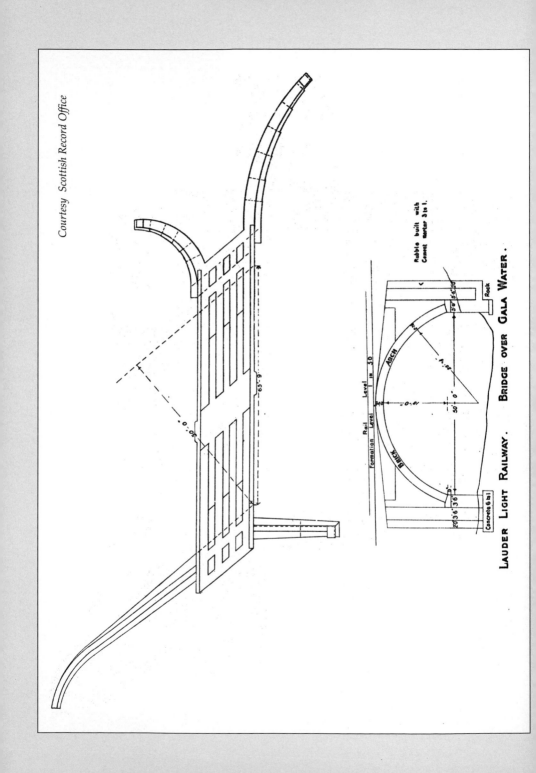

LAUDER LIGHT RAILWAY. BRIDGE OVER GALA WATER.

exceeding at any time twenty-five miles an hour over the portion of the railway within the parish of Lauder or exceeding fifteen miles per hour on any other portion of the railway or exceeding ten miles per hour when such train or engine shall be passing over any curve the radius of which shall be less than nine chains.

The rate of speed of any train or engine approaching and within a distance of three hundred yards of a level crossing over a public road where no gates are erected or maintained across the railway shall not exceed ten miles per hour but the Board of Trade may fix a lower maximum speed in the case of any such level crossing if the view of the railway from the road near the crossing is at any point or for any distance so obstructed as in their opinion to render the higher maximum speed unsafe for the public crossing the road.

The company was authorised to enter into an agreement with the North British Railway as to the operation of the line and ancillary matters, maximum fares and charges were laid down and the capital structure of the company was set out with the proviso that the Berwickshire County Council and Corporation of Lauder were authorised to subscribe up to £15,000 and to gain representation on the Board thereby.

A Schedule was set out at the end of the Order and this provided as follows:

Permanent Way - The rails used shall weigh at least fifty-six pounds per yard.
On curves with radii of less than nine chains a checkrail shall be provided,
If flat-bottom rails and sleepers are used
(a) The rails at the the joints shall be secured to the sleepers by fang or other through bolts or by coach-screws or by double-spikes on the outside of the rail with a bearing-plate: and
(b) The rails on curves with a radii of less than nine chains shall be secured on the outside of the outer rail to each sleeper by a fang or other through bolt or by a coach-screw or by double spikes with a bearing plate: and
(c) The rails on curves with radii of less than nine chains shall be tied to gauge by iron or steel ties at suitable intervals or in such other manner as may be approved by the Board of Trade.
Turntables - No turntables need be provided but no tender- engine shall be run tender foremost at a rate of speed exceeding at any time fifteen miles per hour.
Electrical Communication - If the Board of Trade require means of electrical communication to be provided the Company shall make that provision in such manner as the Board of Trade direct.
Signals - At places where under the system of working for the time being in force trains may meet cross or pass one another there shall be a home-signal for each direction at or near the entrance points. If the home-signal cannot be seen from a distance of a quarter of a mile a distant signal must be erected at that distance at least from the entrance points. The home-signals and distant signals may be worked from the station by wires or otherwise.
Every signal arm shall be weighted as to fly to and remain at danger on the breaking at any point of the connection between the arm and the lever working it.
Precautions shall be taken to the satisfaction of the Board of Trade to ensure that no signal can be lowered unless the points are in the proper position and that two conflicting signals cannot be lowered simultaneously.
Platforms &c. - Platforms shall be provided to the satisfaction of the Board of Trade unless all carriages in use on the railway for the conveyance of passengers are constructed with proper and convenient means of access to and from the same from and to the level of the ground on the outside of the rail.
There shall be no obligation on the Company to provide shelter or conveniences at any

station or stopping place.

Cowcatchers - Every engine used upon the railway where the line is unfenced shall be fitted with a cowcatcher in front and unless turntables are provided every engine shall also be fitted with a cowcatcher in the rear.

Further local agitation took place as a result of which there was a dispute as to what proportion of the capital was to be contributed on behalf of each parish served and what the effect on the local rates would be thereof. There were still some who felt that the proposed line from Dalkeith would be preferable to a branch from Fountainhall and there were others who felt that the terminus of the branch line was too far from the centre of Lauder. Despite these criticisms the new company was formed and on 5th June, 1899 an agreement was reached with the North British Railway in the following terms.

1. That the North British Company shall work and maintain the line for 40 per cent of the gross receipts, provided that if these were less than £10 per mile per week the percentage should be 45 and if less than £8 10s per mile per week it would be 50 per cent.

2. That all receipts in excess of the amount required to pay a dividend of 4 per cent per annum on the authorised share capital of the Lauder Railway were to be divided equally between the North British and Lauder Companies.

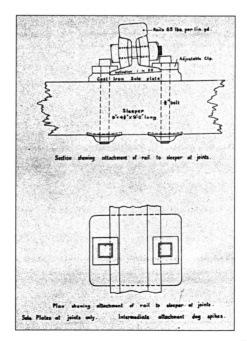

Scottish Record Office

A contract was entered into with Messrs Dick, Kerr & Company, railway contractors of Kilmarnock*, who agreed to construct the line for £34,151 (which included 5 per cent for contingencies) and to supply the permanent way for £5,660. Messrs Blyth and Westland of Edinburgh were appointed as the consulting civil engineers to the project. In May 1899 the company's solicitor was instructed to serve notices for the compulsory purchase of land required by the railway, the estimated value of which was £4,845, and it was said that the line would be open for all traffic within 12 months. The Directors of the new company were the Marquis of Tweedale, the Earl of Lauderdale and Mr George Dalziel, WS, Edinburgh and further Directors were to be appointed on behalf of Berwickshire County Council and Lauder Town Council, the North British Railway and one by the other shareholders of the company. The seal of the company was adapted from the seal of the Burgh of Lauder itself and contained 'a representation of the Virgin standing with the Holy Child in her arms'.†

Of the share capital the North British Railway subscribed £15,000, Berwickshire County Council £12,000, the Lauder Town Council £3,000, the Earl of Lauderdale £500, Lord Tweedale £500, Colonel Hope £500, Mr Tennent, MP, £500, Mr George Rankin, WS, £500, Mr George Dalziel £500, Messrs Blyth and Westland £500, Messrs Miller,Robson & McLean, WS, £500, Mr Thomas Swan, Edinburgh, £500, Messrs Graham, Johnston & Fleming, WS, £500, Lord Tweedmouth, £250, Mr James Swan, Edinburgh, £200, Mr Graham, Lauder, £200, Mr W.D. Aikman, Edinburgh, £200, Mr Rough, Broxburn, £200, Colonel Money, £200 and Messrs Dick, Kerr & Co., £2,500.

An indignant letter in a local newspaper commented that the Earl of Lauderdale would benefit much from the railway and yet had done very little for it. The writer pointed out that the Earl had only taken £500 in shares and had refused even to take the value of his land in shares but had insisted to being paid in cash in contradistinction to Lord Tweedale who had not anything like the same interest in the district but had even taken the value of his land in shares. The letter concluded,

> Your readers outside the Lauder district can now judge of Lord Lauderdale's interest in the railway, and yet I am told a member of his family is to be asked to cut the first sod!

while in another newspaper it was said that

> The people of Lauder themselves have not shown quite so much enthusiasm in subscribing to the capital of the company as might have been expected; they have been somewhat apathetic in the matter, and most of the money has been raised outside of the district. However now that the railway is an assured fact, it is to be hoped that the enthusiasm of the inhabitants of the burgh and the surrounding country will be aroused and that they will heartily support them.

---

* The firm of Dick, Kerr & Co. Ltd, was already well-known as railway contractors and builders of steam locomotives and suppliers of electric tramcars and they operated from the Britannia Works, Kilmarnock and a newly-opened factory in Preston. They later amalgamated with Siemens and others to form the English Electric Company Ltd., now part of GEC.
† The original of this seal is in the Glasgow Museum of Transport; it is reproduced on the title page of this work.

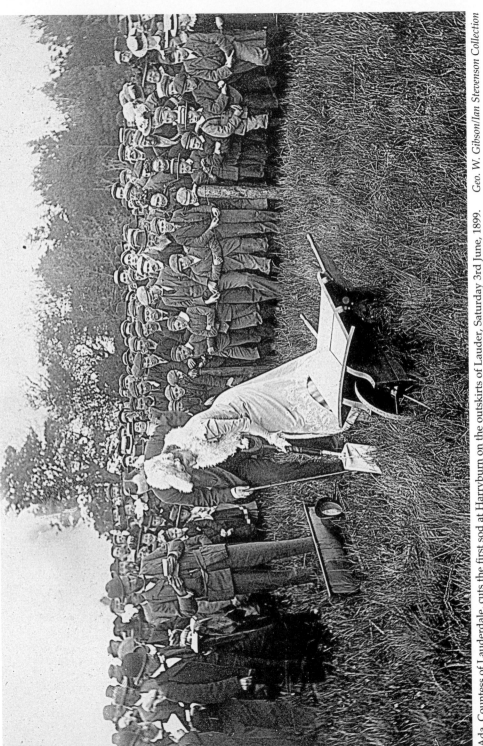

Ada, Countess of Lauderdale, cuts the first sod at Harryburn on the outskirts of Lauder, Saturday 3rd June, 1899.   Geo. W. Gibson/Ian Stevenson Collection

On Saturday 3rd June, 1899 the important ceremony of the cutting of the first sod took place at noon in a field near to Harryburn House at the spot where Lauder station was to be built. The weather was fine and the event was well attended, all business in Lauder being suspended for three hours and several buildings in the town being decorated with bunting. The band of the Lauder Company of Volunteers provided musical entertainment and after a speech from Mr John Kerr, a Director of Dick, Kerr & Co, Ada, Countess of Lauderdale cut the first sod with a silver spade which she had been presented with by the contractors.* After the playing of the National Anthem an excellent luncheon was provided by the contractors for the Earl and Countess and a large company of ladies and gentlemen; the venue of this was the Volunteer Hall which had been profusely decorated for the occasion. Provost Moore of Lauder made a lengthy speech extolling the virtues of the burgh, Mr Hall Blyth, C.E., proposed a toast and there was some good-natured banter to the effect that those present hoped that their railway would be completed before the Gifford and Garvald Railway in neighbouring East Lothian.† Other toasts followed and at intervals in in the proceedings songs were rendered by members of the party.

The enthusiasm and interest generated by the project is well illustrated by a quotation from the contemporary *History of Channelkirk* by the Revd A. Allan (a great supporter of the line):

Nothing has transpired in the valley for centuries to equal in importance, perhaps, the advent of the railway. The situation of Lauderdale cuts it off with all communication from the outside world, except what it affords across Soutra Hill on the west. In winter this means in too many instances, no communication at all, owing to the roads being blocked with snow. The season proves the express need of a change in the distressing inconvenience which the long-continuing storm produces.

On 9th December of last year, 1899, a south-east wind accompanied with frost set in and increased in severity till on the 11th and 12th snow was obstructively lying everywhere. Scarcely any change took place till the later days of March, February having been the wildest month of snowstorms in living memory. As a consequence for several weeks no traffic was possible across Soutra and the Parish suffered in many ways as the trade in this direction is very important.

The railway will minimise our winter solitude and make the valley no longer a land of the weary. It is universally welcomed as a boon of the highest magnitude for the commercial and social advantages which are expected to follow its completion are certain to be both many and great.

---

* This spade, which is of solid silver, was inscribed 'Presented to the Countess of Lauderdale by Messrs Dick, Kerr and Company Ltd., contractors, on the occasion of cutting the first sod of the Lauderdale Light Railway, 3rd June, 1899. Messrs. Blyth and Westland, C.E., Engineers.' It is now on show to present-day visitors to Thirlestane Castle.

† In the event it was, but only by some three months. However it was a cause of great pride that the Lauder line had become the very first new Light Railway in Scotland to be opened to the public. Eventually there were others and by 1914 the full list (with dates of opening) read as follows: Carmylie (1900, a pre-existing line originally used by quarry traffic only), Lauder (1901), Gifford & Garvald (1901), Wanlockhead & Leadhills (1901-2), Dornoch (1902), Fraserburgh & St Combs (1903), Wick & Lybster (1903), Cairn Valley (1905), Strathord & Bankfoot (1906), Maidens & Dunure (1906) and Campbeltown & Macrihanish (1906). All apart from the last were standard-gauge and all but one lost their passenger service before 1939. None survive - a testimony to the fact that the 1896 Act was 'too little, too late'.

Construction got underway rapidly and huts were erected for the workmen, housing 190 men at Fountainhall and 80 at Oxton. Great difficulties were experienced in attracting men to work on the line especially at harvest time and by December 1899 the engineers were able to report that the contractors had made fair progress, that the cuttings and embankments for nearly one half of the line were finished and that the greater part of the rails required had been delivered to Fountainhall station. It was expected that a start would soon be made with the laying of the permanent way. The weather still continued to cause difficulties and in February 1900 parts of the trackbed near to Oxton were threatened by extensive flooding.

Although horse and manpower were extensively used a steam navvy was also employed but much of the work was done in the traditional manner using local labour. One of these local people was Mr Sandy Nisbet, later a shepherd at Addington, who was as a 14 year-old employed as a 'nipper'. His duties included taking the workmen's picks and tools to the local blacksmiths in order to have them resharpened and, on one occasion, carrying explosives from Hartside Quarry some five miles or so to the construction site - a practice which a modern Health and Safety Executive officer would immediately condemn.

A dispute now arose between the Lauder Light Railway Company and the North British Railway in relation to the fixing of the rails to the sleepers and also to the spacing of them. The North British insisted that the sleepers be placed two feet six inches apart whereas the Light Railway Order allowed them to be three feet apart, except in the parish of Lauder where the line speed had been increased to 25 miles per hour. The North British also insisted that a shelter and conveniences be provided for passengers at all stations although the Board of Trade had not required this. They also complained that the facilities of Lauder and Oxton for traffic were insufficient and that the platforms should be extended. The company agreed to make certain modifications and the dispute with the North British appeared to have been settled at least for the moment.

At the fourth half-yearly meeting of the shareholders of the company held in Edinburgh on 27th June, 1900 the Directors expressed disappointment at the slow progress of the work. About two-thirds of the cutting work and embankments had been completed, but the masonry work was far behind and there was a great scarcity of building materials. The Chairman blamed the contractors who stated that the delay had been caused by the scarcity of labourers and that, although they provided hut accommodation for 280 men, they had never been able to have more than 120 on the job at any one time. They had offered nearly one penny an hour more wages than were paid in the district but even that inducement had not brought out a sufficient number. The Directors reminded them that there was a penalty clause in the contract and the contractor pointed out to the company that difficulties had been experienced in getting possession of the land. Also that the effect of the war was that nearly 50,000 men had been taken off their usual work and that had caused a great scarcity of unskilled labour not only in the district but throughout the country.*

---

* The South African War attracted many Scots volunteers and caused a severe labour shortage nationally with a 'knock-on' effect on employment in south-east Scotland which meant that the pool of casual labour virtually dried up. The progress of the War was followed locally with great enthusiasm and both the Relief of Mafeking and the taking of Pretoria were celebrated noisily in the streets of Lauder.

Board of Trade Inspection train at Oxton, 28th June, 1901 - the report prepared by Major Pringle on this occasion (which includes comments about the unfinished nature of the station platform here) is reproduced as Appendix 5. *Scottish Record Office*

Opening day at Lauder showing Drummond 0-6-0T No. 240 (the former *Coatbridge* and. later, *Polton*) which had the honour of drawing the first train. *Public Record Office*

NORTH BRITISH RAILWAY

OPENING OF
LAUDER
LIGHT RAILWAY
FOR TRAFFIC
On TUESDAY, 2nd July 1901

The **LAUDER LIGHT RAILWAY** will be opened for Traffic on **TUESDAY, 2nd JULY 1901**, and the following will be the Train Service until further notice.

WEEK-DAYS.		a.m.	a.m.	p.m.	p.m.	
Edinburgh (Wav.)	leave	6 20	9 27	4 25	6 45	...
Carlisle	,,	4 20		12 45	5 55	...
Hawick	,,	6 0	6 55	2 38	5 18	...
Galashiels	,,	6 50	7 42	3 29	8 0	...
Fountainhall	leave	7 40	10 28	5 10	8 25	...
Oxton	,,	8 14	11 2	5 44	8 59	...
Lauder	arrive	8 27	11 15	5 57	9 12	...

WEEK-DAYS.		a.m.	a.m.	p.m.	p.m.	
Lauder	leave	6 25	9 30	3 3	7 3	...
Oxton	,,	6 38	9 43	3 16	7 16	...
Fountainhall	arrive	7 12	10 17	3 50	7 50	...
Galashiels	arrive	7 56	10 43	4 55	8 19	...
Hawick	,,	8 48	11 29	6 10	9 10	...
Carlisle	,,	10 20	12 50	8 16	12 20	...
Edinburgh (Wav.)	,,	8 26	12 58	4 57	9 p 3	...

In connection with the opening of the Lauder Light Railway the following alterations will come into force, viz.:—
The 9·27 a.m. Train from Edinburgh to Hawick will call at Fountainhall at 10·23 a.m.
The 4·25 p.m. Train from Edinburgh to Carlisle will call at Fountainhall at 5·4 p.m.
The 7·10 p.m. from Kelso to Edinburgh will call at Fountainhall at 8·19 p.m.

Ordinary Fares.

TO	From OXTON.				From LAUDER.			
	Single.		Return.		Single.		Return.	
	First Class.	Third Class.	First Class.	Third Class.	First Class.	Third Class.	First Class.	Third Class.
	s. d.	s. d.	s. d.	s. d.	s. d.	s. d.	s. d.	s. d.
Lauder	0 8	0 4	1 1	0 8	...	...	...	...
Oxton	...	...	...	...	0 8	0 4	1 1	0 8
Fountainhall	1 1	0 6	1 10	1 1	1 9	0 10	2 11	1 9
Galashiels	2 11	1 5	5 1	2 10	3 7	1 9	6 2	3 6
Hawick	6 2	3 0	10 1	6 1	6 10	3 4	11 5	6 9
Carlisle	13 8	6 10	22 10	13 9	11 4	7 2	23 11	11 5
Edinburgh	4 10	2 5	8 4	4 10	5 6	2 9	9 2	5 6
Glasgow	9 10	4 11	15 7	9 10	10 6	5 3	16 8	9 6

EDINBURGH, June 1901.   (12-0)   Hugh Paton & Sons, Printers, Edinburgh.

W. F. JACKSON, General Manager.

Poster advertising the opening of the line - the original is in three colours.

Scottish Record Office

At the following half-yearly ordinary meeting of the company, held in Edinburgh on 26th December, 1900, the Directors regretted that they had again to express disappointment at the progress on the railway during the last six months. The cuttings and embankments on the line were nearly complete but the masonry work had been carried on very slowly and if the weather was at all favourable should be completed within about three months. The laying of the permanent way had been seriously retarded for the want of ballast and only two miles of track had been laid and finished off. The contractors had hitherto been obtaining the whole of their ballast requirement from a small quarry near the works (probably Airhouse) and the Directors of the North British had repeatedly pointed out to them that this was absolutely insufficient. By agreement, however, with the NBR, a temporary junction with the new line had been made at Fountainhall and as a result 15,000 to 20,000 tons of ballast was expected to be brought in from outside sources. It was said that allowances had been made for the deplorable weather conditions and it was hoped that the works would be carried on with a little more energy and activity and that they would be finished within the next three months. It was undoubtedly true that the previous winter had been a bad one and the road from Lauder to Stow had been blocked by drifts for some time while the following spring had been excessively wet, but the Directors remained dissatisfied with the contractors as did the North British.

In the early part of the new year the works continued to progress slowly but on 30th March, 1901 the engineers reported to the North British that 'we expect the line to be opened by 15th May'. Easter passed and it was becoming apparent that the railway would not be opening by May; the North British minutes of the 11th of that month somewhat laconically record that 'The opening of the new line is likely to be delayed for some time yet.' Work progressed and staff appointments were now made and these included Mr Rogers, the booking clerk at Peebles, being appointed as station master at Lauder and Mr Lockhead, spare signalman at Galashiels, being appointed station master of Oxton. On 28th June, 1901 Major Pringle of the Board of Trade made an official inspection of the completed line and found it to be in order* and it was announced that the Lauder Light Railway would be opened to all traffic on Tuesday 2nd July, 1901, there having been insufficient time to issue the necessary notice to staff and the public to have the line opened on Monday 1st as originally intended.

---

* Major Pringle's report, erroneously dated 31st June 1901, is reproduced as Appendix 5.

The first timetable, July, 1901.

A ticket used on the first train - note the comparatively expensive fare.

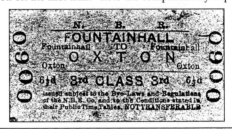

A dividend warrant for Half-Year to 30th June, 1904. The sum of 7s. 2d. represented a dividend at 1½ per cent per annum for the Half-Year on five shares of £10 each less 4d. income tax (levied at the rate of 11½d. in the pound).

Chapter Three

Resource and Enterprise
THE LAUDER LIGHT RAILWAY, 1901-1922

'The puff of 'Billy' in the dale,
The noise of whistle scream,
Reminds us of an enterprise
Which once was but a dream.'
'The Lauder Light Railway'

Amidst great local celebrations, the Lauder Light Railway was opened to the public on Tuesday 2nd July, 1901. The first train out, the 6.20 am from Lauder to Fountainhall, left the terminus with 62 passengers aboard and a further 51 joined the train at Oxton. It was said that these first passengers were most excited about seeing the familiar countryside for the first time out of a carriage window as 'Maggie Lauder', as the diminutive train was immediately christened, rattled her way along the line at something less than breakneck speed. Many special trips were made on the line in that first week and these included the local Sheriff and a party on the Wednesday, a school excursion on the Friday and the first journey over the line by the Earl of Lauderdale on the Saturday. The school trip was described thus in a local newspaper:

The first outing of any association in the district took place on Friday, the 5th July, when the children attending Cleekhimen Public School had their annual trip. Miss Pringle, the school mistress, a young lady of resource and enterprise, left the beaten track this year of a sojourn in the neighbourhood by taking advantage of the railway, whereby the children had an excellent trip across the Gala Water. The idea of a railway excursion which emanated from Miss Pringle, was an excellent one. Most of the children, never had seen a train before,far less having had the pleasure of a ride in one, and it is needless to say they immensely enjoyed the innovation. The children met at the school all bright and happy, and mostly dressed in white, carrying flags, flowers, etc. They were marshalled in order by the mistress, and moved off to Oxton Station to catch the 9.43 am train. Ample provision had been made by the railway company for the accommodation of the children, and when the train moved off ringing cheers were given from the youthful throats in their delight in the prospect of a railway journey. This is the first trip of a school or of any combination that has taken place on the Lauder Light Railway. On arrival at Fountainhall, they were marched from the station to a field on a farm near Fountainhall Station, and on passing the public school there all the scholars turned out and under the direction of Mr King, headmaster, gave the Cleekhimin scholars a hearty welcome. Mr King, in a short speech, congratulated Miss Pringle upon the neat and tidy appearance of the children, and hoped that they would have a happy day beside the Gala Water. Amid ringing cheers from the representatives of both schools, the scholars were marched to their destination and were received at the farm of Mr and Mrs Lumsden and family, who accorded them a hearty welcome. The scene of merrymaking was in close proximity to the railway and Gala Water and the swift passing of the trains on the main line seemed a source of endless delight to the children. The inner wants of the children were admirably attended to, pies and milk being served out in abundance, after which the picnic began in earnest, swings, cricket, racing, etc., being freely engaged in. Tea was served at three o'clock and of this all heartily partook. Before leaving for

LAUDER LIGHT RAILWAY.

WEEK-DAYS. Up Trains.	Distance from Fountain-hall Stn.		1 Pass.	2	3 Pass. Mixed	4	5 Pass. Mixed	6	7	8 Pass Mixed	9	10
	Miles	Chns	a.m.		a.m.		p.m.			p.m.		
Edinburgh (Waverley) ... depart	...	...	6 15	...	9 35	...	4 25	...	...	6 50		...
Galashiels ... ... ,,	...	...	...	...	8 45		3 26	...	...	8 13		...
Fountainhall Station ... depart	...	...	7 34	...	10 33	...	5 8	...	...	8 45		...
Oxton ... ... ,,	6	88	8 2	...	11 1	...	5 36	...	...	9 13		...
Lauder... ... ... arrive	10	33	8 15	...	11 14	...	5 49	...	...	9 26		...

Nos. **5** & **8**.—Do not convey wagons to or from Oxton, except when required, a wagon of Live Stock from Fountainhall to Oxton.

WEEK-DAYS. Down Trains.	Distance from Lauder.		1 Pass. Mixed	2	3 Pass.	4	5 ‡ Pass.	6	7	8 Pass. Mixed	9	10
	Miles	Chns	a.m.		a.m.		p.m.			p.m		
Lauder... ... ... depart	...	...	6 45	...	8 22	...	3 5	...	...	7 14		...
Oxton ... ... ,,,	3	75	6 58	...	8 35	...	3 18	...	...	7 27		...
Fountainhall Station ... arrive	10	33	7 26	...	9 3	...	3 46	...	...	7 55		...
Galashiels ... ... arrive	...	...	7 56	...	10 48	...	4 55	...	...	8 24		...
Edinburgh (Waverley) ... ,,	...	...	8 54	...	9 43	...	4 57	...	...	9 35		...

No. **1**.—Does not convey Wagons to or from Oxton except on Mondays and Tuesdays when it will lift Live Stock at that Station when required. ‡ No. **5**.—Is a mixed Train on Saturdays only. No. **8**.—Does not convey wagons to or from Oxton. Note.—The Branch Engine and Guard will make a Goods trip from Lauder to Fountainhall and back between 11-14 a.m. and 3-5 p.m

Working timetable 1906.

Wartime economies - NBR working timetable, October 1916.

LAUDER LIGHT RAILWAY.

WEEK-DAYS. Up Trains.	Distance from Fountain-hall.		1	2	3 Pass. Mixed	4	5 Pass. Mixed	6	7	8	9	10
	Miles	Chns			a.m.		p.m.					
Fountainhall ... ... depart	...	...	...	...	10 35	...	5 8	...	...	...	...	...
Oxton ... ... ,,	6	88	...	...	11 3	...	5 36	...	...	...	...	...
Lauder... ... ... arrive	10	33	...	...	11 16	...	5 49	...	...	...	...	...

No. **5**.—Does not convey wagons to or from Oxton, except when required, a wagon of Live Stock from Fountainhall to Oxton.

WEEK-DAYS. Down Trains.	Distance from Lauder.		1	2	3 Pass. Mixed	4	5 ‡ Pass.	6	7	8	9	10
	Miles	Chns			a.m.		p.m.					
Lauder... ... ... depart	...	...	...	...	8 10	...	3 5	...	...	...	...	...
Oxton ... ... ,,	3	75	...	...	8 23	...	3 18	...	...	...	...	...
Fountainhall ... ... arrive	10	33	...	...	8 51	...	3 46	...	...	...	...	...

No. **3**.—Does not convey Wagons to or from Oxton except on Mondays and Tuesdays. † This train will be due to arrive Fountainhall 6 minutes later when Live Stock is lifted at Oxton.
‡ No. **6**.—Is a Mixed train on Saturdays only.
Note.—The Branch Engine and Guard will make a Goods trip from Lauder to Fountainhall and back between 11-16 a.m. and 3-5 p.m

LAUDER LIGHT RAILWAY—Week-days.

UP TRAINS. Stations.	Distance from Fountain-hall		1	2 Pass. Mixed	3 Pass. Mixed	4 Pass.	DOWN TRAINS. Stations.	Distance from Lauder.		5	6 Pass. Mixed	7 ‡ Pass.	8 Pass.
	Miles	Chns		a.m.	p.m.	p.m.		Miles	Chns		a.m.	p.m.	p.m.
Fountainhall dep.	...	...	...	9 23	5 10	8 12	Lauder ... dep.	...	...	...	8 10	3 11	6 24
Oxton ... ,,	6	38	...	9 51	5 38	8 40	Oxton ... ,,	3	75	...	8 23	3 24	6 37
Lauder ... arr.	10	38	...	10 4	5 51	8 53	Fountainhall arr.	10	33	...	8 51	3 52	7 5

No. **3**.—Does not convey wagons to or from Oxton, except when required, a wagon of Live Stock from Fountainhall to Oxton.
No. **6**.—Does not convey Wagons to or from Oxton except on Mondays and Tuesdays. † This train will be due to arrive Fountainhall 6 minutes later when Live Stock is lifted at Oxton. ‡ No. **7**.—Is a Mixed train on Saturdays only.
Note.—The Branch Engine and Guard will make a Goods trip from Lauder to Fountainhall and back between 10-4 a.m. and 3-11 p.m.

Post-War restoration - June 1919.

home Mrs Lumsden kindly gave each of the scholars an orange, which was the signal of a fresh outburst of cheers to Mr and Mrs Lumsden and family for the very great kindness they had shown. The children left by the five pm train for Oxton, one and all being highly delighted with this excellent treat, which will long live as a red-letter day in the minds of the whole of them. Miss Pringle, under whose sole direction the trip took place, is to be congratulated upon its grand success, as well as upon her painstaking endeavours for the happiness of the children, and her assiduous and careful attention to their welfare.*

The initial train service consisted of four return services from Lauder to Fountainhall where onward connections were provided to Galashiels and Edinburgh. The first train left Lauder at 6.25 am (giving an arrival in Edinburgh at 8.25 am) and the last at 7.03 pm; there was no Sunday service. The 10 mile journey was accomplished in 47 minutes at an average speed of just over 12 miles per hour, including the intermediate stop at Oxton. The carriages provided for passengers were somewhat elderly four- and six-wheel North British wooden coaches of Drummond or Holmes design with no corridors or lavatory accommodation. The normal make-up of a train would include a brake composite and a third class carriage although the composite was often left off and thereby no first class accommodation was provided. The carriages were unheated and there was no provision for footwarmers in winter, the North British having refused to countenance the expense of providing a boiler at Lauder to heat the water for the same.

An early complaint from a passenger was recorded in the *Scotsman* of 8th August, 1901 when a correspondent advised passengers to supply themselves with a lamp or candles and matches since they would find themselves in total darkness in the carriages. He went on to comment that 'the filthy state of the carriages might also be referred to' - this latter complaint being a recurrent theme in the files of the NBR. In respect of the *Scotsman* complaint, the company claimed that on the day in question the carriage lamps had not been lit 'owing to the high wind in the absence of a proper lamp for the purpose, which has now been sent'. Other contemporary complaints related to the fact that the carriages provided 'were not quite as comfortable as they ought to be' and that there 'were often not enough seats available for passengers', while it was often said that the speed of trains between Oxton and Fountainhall left something to be desired.

The North British Railway was, however, not satisfied with the standard of work which had been carried out by the contractors or with the facilities which had been provided by the Lauder Light Railway Company. On 15th July, 1901 the goods manager of the NBR wrote to his General Manager stating that he was unhappy about the accommodation for dealing with livestock on the branch and said that the loading bank at Lauder was unsatisfactory. He also pointed out that there was a considerable traffic in livestock from Lauderdale to Newcastle and that the rates for conveying that traffic would require careful adjustment, the traffic hitherto having been walked to St Boswells. As he put it, 'It will require a tempting rate to divert it by rail via Fountainhall.'

---

* Miss Isabelle Pringle remained schoolmistress at Cleekhimen until her retirement and some of her former pupils still remember her as 'a very positive and forceful figure'. The little country primary school at Cleekhimen, a couple of miles from both Oxton and Lauder, was closed in the 1960s.

A splendid early view of Fountainhall Junction, *c.* 1904, by Selkirk photographer R. Clapperton, showing the new signal box, an Edinburgh to Galashiels train in the main up platform, a Lauder branch train in the bay and a well-filled goods yard. *R. Clapperton*

Lauder branch train at Fountainhall, *c.* 1903 - the engine is 'R' class 4-4-0T No. 33 (the former *Bellgrove*) - the original plate is, unfortunately, somewhat damaged. *R. Clapperton*

A more serious criticism was reflected in a letter from the consulting engineers to the North British Railway General Manager dated 31st July, 1901 when they stated that,

> Your letter of the 29th correctly states that an engine left the points at the west end of the loop at Oxton Station on the 19th instant owing to defective blades on the points. There is no doubt that some of the ten chain curves have shown a tendency to spread a little, but this is more due to the engine than anything else. The engine was a new one and came straight from the shop at the works and was very hard on the line - in fact it has to be returned to the shop to be altered. We think it would be better if you could arrange to work the line with a bogie engine.

This incident was reported in somewhat different terms by Matthew Holmes, the locomotive superintendent of the North British Railway who claimed that the locomotive involved, No. 313, (one of the Drummond 0-6-0 tank engines and sister to No. 240 which had the distinction of having hauled the first passenger train over the line) had had to be withdrawn to have the flanges of its wheels turned owing to the excessive wear caused by the new rails, sharp curves and the exceptionally dry weather. But he conceded that the 'R' class 4-4-0T engines, one of which was undergoing tests on the Gifford Light Railway, would be more suitable for the Lauder line than the 0-6-0Ts and that the company would try to provide these as soon as possible.

There seems to have been a delay in providing the 4-4-0T as there was a further complaint in October of the same year relating to an 0-6-0 tank, No. 240, which was said to have spread the gauge on part of the line by between three-quarters and seven-eighths of an inch. It was claimed that the average life of an engine on the branch was only about ten days before it had to be returned to the shops for repairs. Once the 4-4-0T engines had arrived the complaints about excessive wear stopped but it is interesting to note that the contractors were eventually awarded the sum of £125 in an arbitration counterclaim against the Lauder Light Railway Company arising out of damage to the track by the use of unsuitable locomotives, and the North British received £150 in compensation for the damage to their locomotives.

In terms of the original agreement between the North British Railway and the Lauder Light Railway (LLR) the NBR were to take over the maintenance of the line one year after its satisfactory completion by the contractors. It was being claimed that the ballasting was sub-standard and that the embankments and cuttings had not been properly finished off. The latter point was reinforced when the embankment near Lauder station subsided after a heavy rainstorm barely a month after the line was opened and remedial works were called for. Another disagreement concerned the fact that the Lauder line was laid with flat-bottom rail - rails with a flat section at their base which enabled them to be fastened direct to the sleepers - as opposed to the then conventional bull-headed rail which was supported in chairs attached to the sleepers. Difficulties were apparently encountered when the gauge of the rails spread and the sleepers then needed continual re-spiking. In a letter dated 10th September, 1901 William Bell, Engineer to the North British Railway, wrote to the NBR General Manager in the following terms:

LAUDER, TRAIN.

R. C. NO. 1120,

Train crossing the Gala Water and heading for the Edinburgh Road level crossing, c. 1903. Note the crossing keeper and his hut, the warning notices and the bicycles belonging to the photographer and his lady friend.

R. Clapperton

Sir, referring to our meeting in connection with the taking over of the maintenance of the Lauder Light Railway - I find after going over the matter carefully that it will cost £608 in wages for the maintenance of this line for the ten months still to run of the contractor's term of maintenance, to this must be added a sum of £902 for lifting, regauging and reballasting giving a total of £1,510; but as I have already mentioned, assuming that the work is carried out with the existing fastenings I am quite satisfied that in a few months the gauge will be as bad as ever and will be a continuing source of worry if not risk, until the line is secured to the sleepers with chairs and spikes. As Mr Blyth explained at the meeting the Lauder Company have positively refused to put down a chaired road and it would be in the interests of this company, seeing that we are to maintain the line, to take over the maintenance at once, as we would then secure the permanent way matters in a much better condition than would do if the contractor maintains the line for the remainder of the term. The estimate of the cost of rechairing the line is to be £2,698 14s. 3d.

While on the subject I cannot express myself too strongly in favour of the chaired road, not only from a permanent way maintenance point of view but also from a rolling stock point of view, independent of the greater security to the traffic; and I think the fact of three or four engines having already been over the line and taken off owing to their tyres having suffered so much corroborates what I say. You are no doubt aware that the Wansbeck Valley Railway* was laid with flat-bottom rails and they all had to be lifted and replaced and that line was worked with a much lighter class of tank engine than the ones on the Lauder Light Railway.

Other correspondence passed between the North British Railway, the contractors and Messrs Blyth and Westland. Typical of these was a letter from the NBR dated 13th August, 1901 which stated:

I am in receipt of your letter of yesterday's date. Am I to understand that you are under the impression that there is no necessity for an office at Oxton, and, if so, how do you suggest we should collect our fares and rates at the place? Surely it is unreasonable to suppose that the work can be conducted without an office?

In a reply two days later Blyth & Westland stated that,

We certainly never anticipated that a booking office would be necessary at Oxton Station. It was intended that the fares and rates at this place should be collected by the guard of the train, as is done at the intermediate stations on the Carmyllie Light Railway.

and a further complaint related to the absence of fire places in the existing buildings. These had been omitted for reasons of cost but after complaints that the signalling block instruments were being adversely affected by damp weather conditions these were installed at a cost of £7 10s. each. The station master at Lauder relayed to the NBR 'numerous complaints' from passengers relating to the lack of public conveniences and platform seats and two of the latter were provided, at the grudging expense of the Lauder company, for 27s. each.

At the LLR half-yearly shareholders' meeting held in December 1902, the attention of the Board was drawn to 'the very narrow and dangerous platform' at Oxton station and the lack of waiting-room facilities there, but it was claimed that this was a matter for the North British since they worked the line. Another complaint subsequently arose in relation to the same station where it was said

---

* This Northumberland branch line was acquired by the North British in 1863. It was closed to passenger traffic in 1952 and to all traffic in 1966.

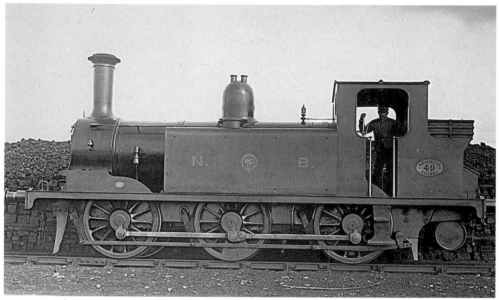

One of the Drummond 'R' class 'Terriers' which operated the line for the first few weeks and had to be replaced owing to the damage which they did to the lightly laid trackwork - this particular example was originally named *Sunnyside* and later *Gretna* and survived until 1924.

Authors' Collection

Lauder station, 1903. The message on the back reads 'Tell mummy and daddy to take a good look at this p.c. and see if they know who is there - it must have been taken that morning you went away from Lauder. I saw it in a shop by accident and think it is so good'. The postmark reads 'Lauder 2.30 PM, SP 24 09' and the recipient lived at Station Cottages, Broughton, Peebleshire.

R. Clapperton

that an old carriage body was required for the storage of sacks and goods, there being no covered accommodation at the station for that purpose. But despite the fact that a proper shed with the same capacity as an old carriage body would have only cost £20, nothing was done and, in 1906, the station master reported that trade was being lost by reason of this absence.

A perennial complaint related to the absence of lighting at stations on the line. In 1903 George Broomfield, a local solicitor, wrote to the North British that the lighting at Lauder station (or, rather, the lack of it!) was 'a disgrace and the talk of the district'. The company investigated the matter and came to the conclusion that the complaint was justified. In an internal memorandum it was said that to light the station with gas would certainly be a great improvement on the oil lamps currently used, 'but the expense is considerable and if it is desirable to curtail expenditure . . . then the matter can quite well stand over.' It was estimated that the cost of lighting the station with oil lamps in the preceding year had been £1 16s. (i.e. the cost of 41 gallons of paraffin oil) but that the cost of installing gas lamps would be £25 and the annual running cost would be £5 5s. The NBR engineer concluded that 'it would be an improvement if the station at Lauder and the approach road were to be lighted with gas. The approach road is about 200 yards long and the public have some difficulty in finding their way in the dark.' An offer by the Lauder Gas Light Company to instal gas at the station was turned down and there the matter was left for the time being.

Traffic seems to have been better than anticipated and in the first three months of operation, after deduction of the NBR share, the LLR traffic receipts amounted to £383 18s. 1d. or almost £30 per week. In the September of that first year 752 tons of goods were dealt with at Lauder and 299 tons at Oxton while a total of 1,300 passengers had been carried on the branch trains that month and 2,046 sheep had been sent from Oxton to main line destinations. This level of traffic held up and the Lauder company continued to pay a steady dividend throughout its independent life.

At about this time, thought was given as to whether or not it would be a worthwhile venture to take a proposal to extend the line in a south-eastern direction so as to give a connection with the Duns to St Boswells line. An earlier proposal, to extend the line to Earlston, was modified and a new scheme was put forward for a line seven miles or so in length which would start at Lauder station, run to the south of the town and then follow the main road and River Leader for some three miles to Birkhill when it would then swing abruptly eastwards following up a side valley and passing Legerwood (where, presumably there would have been a station or siding) and forming a junction with the Duns line about a mile south of Gordon station. Nothing came of this plan, although on paper at least it looked like a sensible proposal, and one can only assume that a realistic view was taken of the traffic potential and of the fact that the motor car was beginning to be seen on local roads.

Throughout the life of the Lauder branch most of its passengers were destined for Edinburgh, but there were few regular passengers and none who could be termed commuters particularly on the 6.15 am early morning service from Lauder. On the return journey, which left Fountainhall at 7.40 am, the

Two souvenir postcards of the Lauder line - the case being carried by the porter is not the infamous tin chest but contains views of Lauder and district.

A. Y. Henry Collection and A.W. Brotchie Collection

mail, parcels, newspapers and perishable goods for Lauder and Oxton were all carried. At Lauder station the mail was collected by a postman and taken in a two-wheeled barrow to the Post Office for sorting while miscellaneous sundry items were delivered by a local carter, Lizzie Wood, with her cart and pony. Lizzie was apparently something of a local 'character' and people became aware of her arrival by the pack of barking dogs which inevitably accompanied her. Mrs Wood later on became a carrier for the LNER, being licensed by the them to operate motor lorries.

Requests were made for a morning service which would depart at a more civilised time and give a convenient arrival in Edinburgh to coincide with the start of normal business hours. The *Scotsman* newspaper contained several letters in support of such an idea. One correspondent expressed the view that,

> I am certain that with a quick service at a reasonable hour the beautiful and health-giving district of Lauderdale would become a favourite summer residence for many who are at present prevented by the absence of such a connection as is now suggested.

and another wrote to say

> I too had the pleasure of residing in the dale this summer, and strong although my passion for the beauty and quietness is, I am afraid it could not survive another season if the same travelling difficulties still exist. A train reaching town at about 9.30 is what is required . . . 'Move with the times' is scarcely to the point - the day of the motor cars for the general public is not yet.

The latter comment was given some credence by the fact that in 1908 Lauder Town Council had apparently resolved to discontinue repairs to the surface of the main road running through the town on the basis that it was now so little used by traffic.

An examination of the early timetables show that the complaints were justified - the second train of the day left Lauder at 9.30 am but the connection to Edinburgh did not arrive in the capital until 12.58 pm, prompting local comment that it would be quicker to cycle there. There were two further trains at 3.3 pm and 7.3 pm. The best return journey time was provided by the 4.25 pm from Edinburgh whose connection arrived back at Lauder at 5.57, giving a total journey time of 92 minutes from the capital compared with the 208 minutes to Edinburgh taken by the 9.30 am train and its connection at Fountainhall. This basic service pattern remained remarkably constant, two morning and two afternoon return journeys being the norm until the advent of World War I.

An interesting example of the somewhat cavalier nature of the North British and its apparent disregard for passengers is illustrated by a complaint made in December 1907. One wonders whether the NBR's more-publicity conscious rival, the Caledonian, would have treated the public in quite the same way. It concerned a shooting party bound for Oxton who arrived at Fountainhall from Edinburgh only to find that the Lauder train had already left minutes before and, there being a long gap in the timetable before the next train, were then forced to walk a long distance in very cold weather conditions.

Two views of 'R' class 4-4-0T No. 103 *Montrose* - this engine worked the Lauder line in its early days. Note the livery variations.

Authors' Collection

On being expostulated with, the Fountainhall station master stated that he had been severely reprimanded for having, on some occasions, detained the Lauder train a few minutes. Would it be believed that (as we were informed later) this train had that morning been despatched with *not one* passenger aboard while passengers who had received their tickets at Waverley, without any warning that they might lose a connection were quietly steaming into the station ten minutes behind time? *O tempora, o mores.* Now sir, I would like to know by what rights, legal or moral, a railway company has to play with the time and comforts of the travelling public in this fashion. A grosser case of carelessness and discourtesy has, I venture to say, seldom been met with.

Tourists were also catered for. At Lauder a new Temperance Hotel had been erected shortly before the opening of the railway and another new hotel, the Tower, was opened in Oxton village in 1903. One of the chief attractions was the River Leader itself, of which it was said 'no finer trouting stream enters the Tweed'. Cheap day tickets were issued and day trippers became increasingly common. Local guidebooks began to appear and one of the more enthusiastic said:

Though the Lauder Light Railway is comparatively short, the passenger may have in view several scenes of more than local and temporary interest. Channelkirk Church and Manse will call to mind the shepherd lad who watched his flocks on the slopes of the Leader and beheld the glory of Aidan as he joined the angelic choir. He may catch a glimpse of the road by which Johnny Cope fled to Coldstream, and Bonnie Prince Charlie led his leal-hearted Highlandmen. He may, between trains, spend a few hours at Oxton to visit Cross-chain-hill, along the pilgrims' road as far as the Church of the Holy Trinity. And if he be not ecclesiastic, historian, or antiquarian, let him proceed to the terminus, where he may wander for a week of days on Lauder Common, amid 'bonnie braes and wimpling burns,' and inhale the invigorating breeze from the wild and stormy Lammermoors. If he be too old or too lazy to climb, let him in the morning set his watch by the Tolbooth Clock, during the day let him watch the shadows of the 'ill-fated favourites' as they sport on the pellucid Leader under the Castle Bridge, and in the evening let him have a few choice burghers in 'my favourite shop' to pass the gossip of the town. And if all these fail to heal his disordered mind, let him make straight endeavour to discover his relationship that idle writer who gave the name of 'Sleepy Hollow' to one of the most picturesque and pleasing scenes of the Scottish Lowlands. This done, with ticket and baggage he must needs take an early train, and return to that fool's paradise from whence he came.

Another locally produced guide to Lauder commented that,

The railway has proved of great benefit to the district and has been the method of opening up Lauderdale to a large number of visitors. While speed is perhaps not excessive, all admit that the railway is a vast improvement on the old method of travelling.

The fruits of this tourism could be seen locally and a number of families from Edinburgh and further afield would come to spend their summer holidays in the area, taking a house for a fortnight or a month for that purpose. Often the father of the family would travel to his work in Edinburgh on a Monday morning and return on a Friday evening while a further useful source of

NBR Staff on the Lauder Light - the upper view shows Oxton *c.* 1902, the lower Lauder in 1930.
Authors' Collection

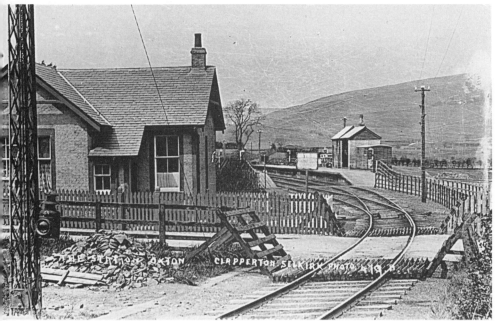

Two early views of Oxton - the station house still survives and the lower postcard is addressed to Lizzie Wood, the railway carter.   *R. Clapperton and Authors' Collection*

The horse and cart belonging to Lizzie Wood, the Lauder railway carter. Miss Wood was noted for her eccentricity but her business managed to survive well into the motor age.
Jackson Collection/Glasgow University

revenue was the special round-trip trains run to Lauder and Earlston for those wishing to explore 'the Scott Country.'

Goods traffic on the line was varied in nature and was normally carried on the pick-up goods train which arrived at Lauder at about mid-day. The principal loads carried were coal, fertilisers and other agricultural requisites inward and livestock and produce outwards. An extremely important traffic was that in sheep although the absence of a direct line from Lauder and Oxton to Newton St Boswells, where the marts were situated, tended to discourage this traffic to some extent. A special service was run on Tuesday mornings for livestock in connection with the weekly market held on that day at Gorgie in Edinburgh. Both Oxton and Lauder stations had cranes and were capable of handling most types of traffic and coal depots were established at the stations. At Lauder the depots were tenanted by Mr Thomas Frater, coal merchant, (succeeded by a Mr Beveridge and Mr Middlemiss) and by the Lothian Coal Company Limited. The two principal customers for coal at Lauder appear to have been the Gas Works and Thirlestane Castle and the traffic in coal over the line was such that Oxton station handled an average of about eight full 10-ton wagons of it every month and Lauder about twenty-six. Wagon loads of coke were sent to the baker at Oxton and these were transhipped at the station to a horse and cart for the short journey up the village street.

There were two sidings situated on the line between Fountainhall and Oxton namely Middleton and Hartside. The former was a private siding for the benefit of tenants at Middletoun Farm and the original lessee was a Mr James Steadman. Hartside served the farm of that name tenanted by James Bertram and also the farm at Threeburnford tenanted by James Fortune, in addition to a quarry situated close by. As a result of this Hartside siding handled a great volume of traffic in stone, albeit on a somewhat sporadic and variable basis while Middleton had a lower volume of steady traffic for many years. All trains on the branch were nominally mixed (i.e. they could convey goods wagons if necessary) but in practice goods were dealt with by a separate working and, due to the lack of a turntable at the terminus, locomotives worked bunker first on the return journey.

In the days at the end of the Edwardian era there was a certain amount of industrial unrest and this culminated in the great miners' strike of 1912 when all passenger train services over the Lauder Light Railway were suspended with effect from Monday 11th March. But as from 13th April a modified service of two trains per day, leaving Lauder at 8.22 am and 4.15 pm and returning from Fountainhall at 10.35 am and 5.08 pm, was introduced pending the restoration of the full service. The LLR shareholders' dividend for the half-year in which the strike occurred was the only pre-war occasion when it fell to below one per cent.

The effect of World War I was profound - many local men and boys left Lauderdale by train never to return and local railwaymen volunteered for active duty despite the fact that they were in a reserved occupation. As an economy measure to conserve both coal and manpower the train service on the line was cut back to two daily return workings, the service not being increased again until after the war. Wages rose rapidly and in 1917 train fares were

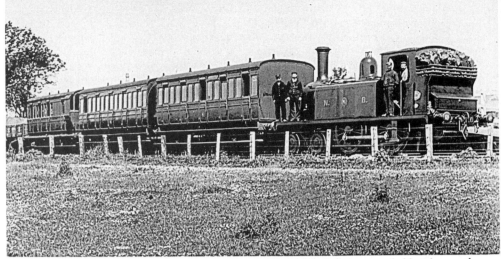

The essence of an NBR branch line train - this pre-World War I shot was probably taken on the Carmyllie Light Railway but the train typifies the era of the light railway in Scotland and trains such as this would have been a familiar sight to travellers on the Lauder line.   *J. Hay Collection*

Train *en route* from Lauder to Oxton, *c.* 1902. Although the original of this photograph is in poor condition the view is an unusual one and the train possesses the character of a tin-plate toy rather than the real thing!   *Ian Stevenson Collection*

increased by 50 per cent across the board. There was however an increase in certain kinds of goods traffic, particularly in locally grown timber required for mining pit props. A government agency, the Timber Supply Department, purchased the Norton, Bullion and Ollister plantations (lying just under a mile north-east of Lauder) from Viscount Maitland of Thirlestain in 1918 and a temporary tramway just under one mile long was constructed to facilitate the felling of the trees there.

One interesting incident occurred in 1919 when one of the regular drivers on the line clyped (*anglice* shopped) on another, claiming that he was often drunk on duty and that on a particular occasion he was said to have given a lift on the footplate of the engine to a local farmer who rewarded him with a bottle of whisky. It was then claimed that the driver in question promptly drank the entire contents of the bottle *en route* with the result that he became so intoxicated by the time that the train arrived at Fountainhall he had to be hidden away from the station master there! His fireman subsequently took the train back to Lauder on his own. The matter reached the attention of Walter Paton Reid, the locomotive superintendent of the North British, who carried out an investigation but no clear conclusion could be drawn as the alleged incident had occurred some time before and it was admitted that there was 'bad blood' between the two drivers. The company decided to settle the issue by giving a strict warning to both of them.

For the duration of the war Britain's railways remained in the control of the Railway Executive although the North British continued to run the service. Changes were however in the air and in the early post-war period there was talk of nationalisation and rationalisation of the many independent railway companies which existed in the country at that time. Eventually the matter was resolved by the Railways Act 1921 which set up four large combines. Both the North British Railway and the Lauder Light Railway were destined to form part of the London & North Eastern Railway company, which was to have a monopoly on railway transport in the east of Britain. Before this took place the Lauder Light Railway Company was awarded a total of £1,670 5s. 8d. compensation in respect of their claim of loss of revenue during the period of Executive control.

In the last period of its independent existence the traffic receipts for the Lauder Light Railway Company in the half-year ending 30th June, 1922 amounted to £1,362 5s. 10d. made up as follows:

	£	s.	d.
Passengers (first-class) (71)	4	4	2
Passengers (third-class) (9,168)	266	16	0
Passengers (Season Tickets) (11)	12	9	7
Parcels Mail & Merchandise	110	12	9
Goods	785	17	9
Livestock	71	8	8
Minerals	21	8	1
Coal	89	8	10

Two private owner wagons used to carry coal on the Lauder Light - both the Lothian Coal Co. and A. & G. Anderson distributed coal via the line to local customers.   *HMRS Collection*

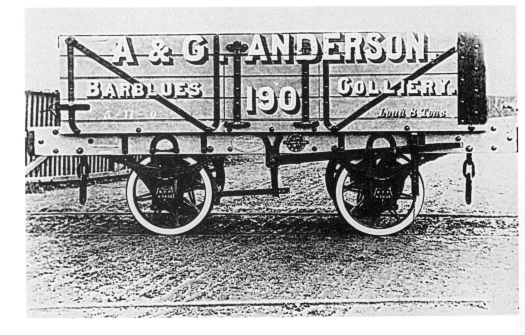

The terms for the absorption of the Lauder Light Railway by the LNER were that (a) £15,000 of preferred ordinary stock of the LNER was to be paid in exchange for the £47,090 ordinary shares of the Lauder Light Railway Company, subject to a proposed reduction in respect of paying the holders of 25 shares or less of the Lauder Company in cash at the rate of £3 2s. 6d. per £10 share, (b) to accept responsibility for loans amounting to £13,500 and (c) to pay the Secretary of the Lauder Company £150 compensation in respect of loss of office. Notwithstanding the dissappearance of the Lauder Light Railway as a separate entity, however, the annual accounts of the Ettrick and Lauderdale District Council still made references to the company throughout the 1980s - the reason for this is not immediately apparent!

It is interesting to note that virtually all of the original shareholders (or if dead their executors) still featured in the Share Register at the end of the company's life and that the Directors of the company had remained virtually unchanged for the last 10 years of the company's existence. The Chairman was the 11th Marquis of Tweedale (who had succeeded to that position on his father's death), the Deputy Chairman was H.G. Younger (a Director of the famous family brewers and a Director of the NBR), and the other Director was Mr R. Dickinson, one of the largest farmers in the Borders, who lived locally at Longcroft. The dividend paid to shareholders had been 1½ per cent until December 1905 and thereafter 1 or 1¼ per cent until 1921 and then fluctuating until a final dividend of 4¼ per cent was paid. Considering the not altogether promising financial nature of the traffic on the line, the shareholders had, all things considered, not done too badly and on 1st January, 1923 the line passed out of local control and the 'Auld Lauder Licht' was finally extinguished.

After the grouping the Drummond 4-4-0Ts became the LNER 'D51' class and continued to run over the line albeit with a new livery and number scheme. Here No. 10462 (the former *Dirleton* which started its life on the Drem to North Berwick branch) is seen at Lauder on 24th August, 1926. *Dr R.A. Read*

An unidentified 'D51' in early LNER days seen on a rather bleak winter day in the bay platform at Fountainhall. *R.W. Lynn Collection*

Chapter Four

London & North Eastern
THE LAUDER BRANCH, 1923-1947

'It's not exactly what we hoped,
Its pace is rather slow'
It taketh 'Billy' all his time
From Fountain Hall to go.'
'The Lauder Light Railway'

Changes were already in the air when the new London & North Eastern Railway took over the line and although outward signs of the new ownership were few, and largely limited to the repainting of the small 4-4-0 tank engines into a new livery and the very gradual appearance of the new initials on rolling stock and publicity, it was already becoming apparent that the 'horseless carriage', dismissed as being a thing of the future barely 20 years ago, was now threatening to become a serious rival to the line.

The reasons for this challenge were not hard to find. A surplus of army trucks left over from the War and a large number of ex-servicemen able to drive helped to make the public aware of the fact that the age of the motor vehicle had arrived. The first local manifestations of this had been largely confined to the appearance of a handful of cars owned by the gentry and rich but there was still little through traffic on the main road through Lauderdale and the railway company managed to retain its precarious monopoly throughout its days of independence. Things were, however, destined to change rapidly within less than a decade.

One of the earliest goods motor vehicles in Lauder had been that of Messrs A. & J. Rutherford, who from about 1912, had delivered goods locally by means of a Model 'T' Ford van. Immediately after the War a new local haulage business, J. & G. Campbell of Oxton, was started up, initially with a horse and cart used to convey road metal from Hartside to Soutra and then with a Foden steam lorry supplemented, in time, by a variety of petrol and diesel lorries including Leylands and Bedfords. Such was the success of Campbell's business that by the 1930s they were carrying a considerable traffic including stone, coal and livestock to local markets, animal feedstuffs from the Chancelot Mills in Leith, and timber, much of this traffic having been abstracted from the railway. Ownership of motor vehicles was, however, still far from universal and local farms such as Middletoun still used the railway for virtually all their requirements.

In 1924 a local entrepreneur, George Deans, announced that he would commence running a public motor bus service from Lauder to Edinburgh via Dalkeith leaving Lauder at 1 pm and returning from the bus stance in Chambers Street, Edinburgh at 6.30 pm at a return fare of 7s. 6d. The initial service was altered to a Tuesday service leaving Lauder at 9.30 am and Edinburgh at 4.30 pm and an additional Thursday service. Mr Deans' bus, known as 'Midside

'Maggie Lauder' in all her glory - the branch train at Fountainhall prior to departure on 24th August, 1927. These were the carriages in which the Heriot's schoolboys did their homework and from which the country people and day-trippers watched the panorama of the changing seasons in the hills and dale.

W.E. Boyd/Scottish Record Office

Maggie' (after a legendary local heroine, Maggie Hardie, the name being caried in large letters on the side of the bus), was often driven by one of Mr Deans' daughters. It seems to have made a sufficient impact locally in that it is still well remembered locally nearly 70 years after its demise. The service flourished and on 1st August, 1927 the rapidly expanding Scottish Motor Traction Company Ltd acquired George Deans' bus and began a direct SMT bus service from Chambers Street, Edinburgh to Lauder, Earlston and Jedburgh. Some services to Jedburgh made the short diversion up the main road from Carfraemill to Oxton village - this facility survives to the present day despite the fact that it involves a quarter-mile diversion and an awkward reversal in the main street of the village.

The following year a joint SMT - United Automobile service from Edinburgh to Newcastle via Lauder and Jedburgh was commenced and this had the doubly unfortunate effect not only of challenging the Lauder branch line for local traffic to Edinburgh (where the journey was both quicker and cheaper by bus, but also involved a lesser mileage and no change *en route*) but also giving a direct service to the Borders and England. If any one single event contributed to the success of the new bus service it was probably the effect of the General Strike of 1926 which led to a complete cessation of all services on the line for some two weeks and thereafter to the introduction of a limited goods service for a further fortnight. The strike showed the public that the railway was not indispensible and that the bus could and would cope easily with the extra traffic - an effect which many local traders were also aware of.

Praise for the bus services was by no means universal - Lauder shopkeepers who had damned the railway for making it possible for locals to buy their messages in Edinburgh now rued the competition which the bus made possible, particularly since the fare had been lowered to 4s. 6d. return (a fare with which the railway could not compete) - at a later date it was possible on a Saturday to hire a taxi and go to Edinburgh to shop at an inclusive fare of only 7s. 6d., which caused the LNER to introduce special Saturday return fares such as a 2s. 6d. return from Oxton to Edinburgh. Even with fares and facilities such as these it was becoming increasingly obvious that the passenger service over the Lauder Light was doomed, notwithstanding the fact that the LNER was itself a major joint shareholder in the SMT company.

One of the weaknesses of the Lauder branch at that time, and indeed one shared in general by railways throughout Britain, was that it was labour intensive and thus expensive to operate. By way of example at Lauder in the 1920s the station staff consisted of H. Wilson, station master, A. Rutherford, clerk and D. Murray and J. Cowan, porters. There were two regular branch crews namely R. Renwick and G. Brown, drivers and L. Whellans and J. Milton, firemen and A. Brown as the engine cleaner. There were two guards, R. Wilson and T. Gall, a coal agent T. Davidson and three surfacemen (permanent way staff) to look after the line, namely W. Brown, D. Fairbairn and C. Graham.

Goods traffic nevertheless held up. The siding at Middleton continued to be used by the Steadman family and later by the Elliots. The principal traffics handled here were sheep and agricultural produce along with miscellaneous traffic such as a horse which was sent by rail on a complicated cross-country

No. 10427 seen in the snow at Lauder in 1930 – this photograph originally accompanied an article on the line which appeared in the *Railway Magazine* in 1931 and which brought this somewhat obscure line to the attention of a wider public.
C. Hamilton Ellis/J. Minnis Collection

journey from here to a farm in Northumberland. Further down the line at Hartside traffic continued to be handled from and to the farms at Hartside and Kirktonhill and Threeburnford and from Airhouse Quarry. Additional traffic was provided by visiting hunts such as the Lauderdale and Roxburgh. On one occasion while the latter were in the area, one of the hunt members, a retired major from the First War, having mislaid his false leg found it necessary to have a replacement limb sent from his home at Cornhill to Oxton - presumably one of the more esoteric items carried over the line.

At Oxton and Lauder goods traffic seems to have peaked in the mid-1920s. Livestock remained the predominant traffic and there are still those who remember the large numbers of sheep, each group being kept a hundred yards apart from the other, which lined the road to Oxton station in the early hours of the market days patiently waiting to board the trains that would take them off to Gorgie market and their eventual doom. In winter there was extra traffic for Newtown St Boswells market (this traffic tending to be walked by road in the summer) and livestock trains were then occasionally operated by two locomotives, one heading the train and one banking at the rear in order to help the heavy load over the line's summit.

Passenger traffic continued in much the same mode as it had done in pre-war days and the relatively few regular passengers travelled in the comfortable but ageing six-wheeled carriages. Trippers, shoppers and others came and went on the three daily services augmented by an evening train on Saturdays which allowed tourists and daytrippers to return from Lauder at 7.14 pm and those in business or pleasure in Edinburgh to return to Lauder at 8.46. One feature of the latter train was that at both Oxton and Lauder many would await it in order to share in its valuable cargo - the 'Pink Edition' of an Edinburgh evening newspaper giving up-to-date football results in an era when the wireless was still uncommon. The ensuing cigarette ends littering the station approach roads would later provide a silent testimony to this important social event. Other passenger traffic was of a more varied nature and included excursion traffic, daytrippers and two distinguished travellers, the composer Ralph Vaughan Williams, who came to visit his aunt at Thirlestane Castle on several occasions, and the railway historian Hamilton Ellis, who travelled over the line in 1929 and whose short account of that journey appears in the *Railway Magazine* of January 1930. He describes the passenger stock as being 'very comfortable in both classes, fitted with steam heating and incandescent gaslight.'

Another passenger albeit deceased was Gwendoline, Countess of Lauderdale, (Vaughan Williams' aunt) who was brought back to Thirlestane from Fort Lauderdale in Florida, where she had died, in a glass-topped lead coffin which was placed on view at Lauder station and later at the castle. On a happier note through excursion trains were regularly run in May and September to the seaside at Portobello, near Edinburgh, at a return fare of 3s. 6d. The story of the small boy who thought that he had missed the train home and began to walk along the East Coast main line from Portobello until stopped by a signalman, whom he then informed that he was intending to walk back to Oxton, was recounted to the authors by the by-now grown-up 'small boy'. These excursions were very popular locally and at least latterly non-corridor bogie

Fountainhall station showing the up platform and Lauder branch bay and signals, *c*. 1920.
Authors' Collection

Fountainhall *c*. 1910 showing the main buildings on the down side and the level crossing. Note the 'Change for Oxton and Lauder' sign below the running-in board.   *Authors' Collection*

Fountainhall *c*. 1952 from the Lauder branch - note the resignalling works in progress.
John Robertson/J.L. Stevenson Collection

Fountainhall - up platform from the level crossing, 27th June, 1955.　　　　*A.G. Ellis*

LAUDER LIGHT RAILWAY.

UP TRAINS.		Distance from Fountain-hall.		WEEK-DAYS.			DOWN TRAINS.		Distance from Lauder.		WEEK-DAYS.		
				1 Goods	2 Goods	3 ...					1 Live Stock	2 Goods	3 ...
CLASS				D	D		CLASS				D	D	
		M.	C.	T O a.m.	M W F O p.m				M.	C.	a.m. T O	M W F O p.m.	
—Fountainhall ...dep.		...	...	7 35	12‡25	...							
Middleton Siding ... „		2	11	......	......	......	—Lauder ... ...dep.		...	...	8 40	2 5	......
Hartside Siding ... „		4	53	...	...	...	—Oxton... ... ... „		3	75	9 0	2 30	......
—Oxton ... ... „		6	38	......	1 30	......	—Fountainhall ... arr.		10	33	9 30	3 ‡ 0	...
Lauder ... arr.		10	33	8 15	1 40	...							

No. 2.—‡ Leaves Galashiels 11.30 a.m. Worked by Galashiels No. 1 Pilot Engine and Guard..

See Note on page 80 *regarding* Live Stock from Lauder Branch to Gorgie Markets.

No. 2.—‡ Arrives Galashiels 4.0 p.m.

Live Stock from Lauder Branch to Gorgie Markets.
On Tuesdays special service to be provided by Galashiels No. 1 Pilot to work Live Stock from Lauder and Oxton to connect at Fountainhall with 7.20 a.m. T O Live Stock train, Kelso to Gorgie.

LNER working timetable, September 1935.

LNER public timetable, Spring 1936.

Table 233. FOUNTAINHALL AND LAUDER.

THE PASSENGER TRAIN SERVICE HAS BEEN WITHDRAWN FROM OXTON AND LAUDER, BUT PARCELS AND MISCELLANEOUS PASSENGER TRAIN TRAFFIC PREVIOUSLY DEALT WITH AT THESE STATIONS WILL CONTINUE TO BE ACCEPTED.

Omnibus services operated jointly by the Scottish Motor Traction Company, Ltd., and the United Automobile Services, Ltd., between St. Boswells, Lauder and Oxton, and by the Scottish Motor Traction Company, Ltd., between Galashiels, Melrose, Earlston and Lauder, are available. For particulars of these services apply to the Station Masters or to the Scottish Motor Traction Company, Ltd., 29, Market Street, Galashiels (Telephone : Galashiels 337).

For train service to and from Galashiels, Melrose and St. Boswells, see Tables 219 and 230.

LAUDER LIGHT RAILWAY

UP TRAINS WEEKDAYS

Distance from Fountainhall		No.	538‡	562											
		Description													
		Class	D	D											
M. C.			Q TO am	SX am											
		Fountainhall........(T) ..	7 35	10F35	....	....									
2 11		Middleton Siding	..	..	..	..	..	..	..	..	..	..	..	..	
4 53		Hartside Siding													
6 38		Oxton .. ..(T) ..	..	11 25	..	..	..	..	..	..	..	..	..	..	
10 33		Lauder	8 15	11 35	....	....									

DOWN TRAINS WEEKDAYS

Distance from Lauder		No.	517	533											
		Description	Live St'k												
		Class	D	D											
M. C.			Q TO am	SX PM											
		Lauder	8 40	12 5	....	....									
3 75		Oxton .. ..(T)..	9 0	12 25	..	..	..	..	..	..	..	..	..	..	
10 33		Fountainhall ......(T)..	9F30	12F50	....	....									

No. 562—F Leaves Galashiels 9.45 a.m. Worked by Galashiels No. 1 Pilot Engine and Guard.

Nos. 517 and 533—F Arrive Galashiels 10,40 a.m. and 1.30 p.m. respectively.

LNER working timetable, October 1945.

stock was used on them. It is said that the LNER encouraged this traffic greatly, especially when the ordinary passenger service was in its final days, and at least one such excursion seems to have been run after the withdrawal of the normal service since some 384 passenger journeys are recorded after 1932. On other occasions Lauder to Fountainhall specials were run for events such as the Gala Show and these were timed to give good connections with Waverley Route services.

The excursion traffic was, of course, not all one way for Lauder was in itself something of an attractive picnic and day-trip venue from Edinburgh and for many years there was a regular 'path' in the timetable for such trains, which were for private parties and were known as 'guaranteed excursions' as the promoters had to pay a certain amount to the company irrespective of patronage - the empty stock would leave from Craigentinny Sidings at 8.10 am. The full train left from No. 3 platform at Waverley at 8.58, the excursions would arive at Lauder at 10.28 and the return journey would leave Lauder at 8.20 pm, arriving at Waverley at 9.47 pm. Two typical examples scheduled for June 1926 included, on Saturday 5th, a special for the employees of W. & M. Duncan,* and on the following Saturday a special for the Edinburgh Corporation Electricity Department's employees.

Throughout the 1920s and early 1930s a small band of commuters used the branch line - these were the group of local boys who attended George Heriot's School† in Edinburgh. Every weekday morning David Harvey (later schoolmaster of Westruther and Lauder), Douglas Gillespie, Jack McLachlan and Richard Renwick (son of one of the engine drivers) travelled up to school on the 6.15 am from Lauder. Often they were the only passengers on the train, apart from the sheep and cattle whose wagons were attached at Oxton on Tuesday and Thursday market days. The schoolboys came to know and like every inch of the route and they have the distinction of being, apart from the railway staff, the most travelled passengers on the Lauder Light. They used to do their homework in the rattling wooden carriages although it must be said that the jolting of the train made writing difficult. They were well known to the staff and the train, on occasions, would wait for a late straggler while at other times they were allowed to travel in first class compartments, the guard's van and even, as a special treat, on the footplate of the engine. Other occasional passengers on the early train included Jim Moffat, the railway fencer, and Mr Leeming, the LNER molecatcher. On the second Monday in May and September extra coaches were attached and run through to Edinburgh for the crowds of people who took advantage of the local holiday in order to travel up to the capital - much to the chagrin of the Heriot's pupils whose school took Edinburgh holidays only, these being on different dates.

* Duncans were famous for 'walnut whips' and other chocolate products and for many years sent up to 20 tons of goods per week by rail from their Canonmills, Edinburgh, factory (opened in 1900) to Liverpool and Glasgow. Taken over by Rowntrees and later independent again, they still produce confectionery although no longer in Edinburgh and no longer sent by rail.

† Founded in the 17th century by King James VI's jeweller, the school (now co-educational) still occupies its splendid original buildings. The reason for such a long journey was (apart from the reputation of the school itself and the generous bursaries then given to country boys) that the only local senior secondary school was Duns High which involved a five mile cycle run to Earlston followed by a long train journey with the disadvantage of arriving late at school and of having to leave early.

> # PASSENGER RAIL FACILITIES WITHDRAWN
>
> The L.N.E.R. intimate that on and after Monday, September 12, passengers will not be conveyed to and from Oxton and Lauder stations on the Fountainhall-Lauder branch railway. Omnibus services by the S.M.T. Company will be available between Galashiels, Melrose, and Lauder, and the S.M.T. Company and United Omnibus Co. joint services will also be available between Edinburgh, Lauder, and St Boswells. Oxton and Lauder stations will still be open for the acceptance and delivery of parcels and other passenger main traffic, and the present facilities for the conveya' of goods traffic will be continued.

The withdrawal of passenger services as reported in *The Scotsman*, Monday, 29th August, 1932.

Circular issued to LNER staff advising of withdrawal of passenger services on the branch.

LONDON & NORTH EASTERN RAILWAY.

Circular $\frac{G. M.}{238}$

GENERAL MANAGER'S OFFICE
(SCOTLAND),
EDINBURGH, *2nd September* 1932.

Withdrawal of Passenger Train Services on Gullane and Lauder Branches.

The Staff are hereby informed that on and after Monday, 12th September 1932, the Passenger Train Services will be withdrawn from the undernoted Stations :—

Gullane Branch.	Lauder Branch.
Aberlady.	Oxton.
Gullane.	Lauder.

Detailed instructions relating to Parcels and Goods Traffic will be issued in due course by the Officers concerned.

J. CALDER,
General Manager (Scotland).

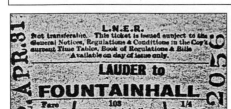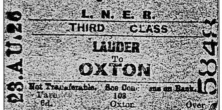

Tickets issued for travel on the branch in LNER days.

The number of passengers carried over the line continued to fall sharply and by 1931 Oxton station was handling an average of only 23 passengers per week (or less than one per train!). Lauder's total was little better and in both cases the figures were less than one-quarter of what they had been only a few years before. The end of the passenger service was now inevitable. Preliminary surveys were carried out and the question was mooted as to whether or not any savings could be made by replacing the conventional passenger service with a Sentinel steam railcar* but, since a single engine handled both goods and passenger services over the branch, it was felt that no such savings could be made. A memorandum was then prepared by the General Manager of the Scottish Area of the LNER, James Calder, and sent to the Traffic, Locomotive and Works Committees of the company for their comments. The memorandum, dated 12th July, 1932, read as follows:

CLOSING OF BRANCH LINES - LAUDER LIGHT RAILWAY
SCOTTISH AREA

The passenger traffic on the Lauder Light Railway, which has been falling away for a number of years as a result of road competition, has now declined to such an extent that the passenger Train service can no longer be justified, and it is not anticipated that it will be possible to recover the traffic to rail.

The Branch, which consists of about 10½ miles of single track, extends from Fountainhall Junction, on the Edinburgh and Carlisle main line, to Lauder, and serves an agricultural district by stations located at Oxton and Lauder. One engine undertakes both the Goods and Passenger services meantime, and the introduction of a Sentinel Cammell Car would not admit of further economies, as the present engine would in any case be required for working the goods traffic.

No case arises for closing the line entirely as the Goods traffic continues to be well maintained and it is estimated that about 75 per cent of the parcels traffic could be retained if catered for by Goods train.

In the event of the Passenger trains being withdrawn, a saving estimated at £1,273 per annum could be effected to the Company, as under:

Savings	Per annum	
Maintenance of Way and Works	£ 133	
Maintenance and Renewal of Carriages	£ 222	
Locomotive Department	£ 869	
Traffic Expenses	£ 495	
Miscellaneous	£ 20	£1,739
Loss in Revenue		
Passengers	£ 349	
Parcels	£ 105	
Miscellaneous	£ 12	£ 466
Net Saving		£ 1,273

There is no legal objection to the withdrawal of the Passenger trains and as an adequate service of Road Omnibuses is provided in the district by the Scottish Motor Traction Co. Ltd, it is not anticipated that any serious complaints will arise from the public.

* These early forerunners of the ubiquitous post-war diesel multiple unit were used by the LNER and the LMS on a number of Scottish branch lines including the Selkirk branch.

Snow in the hills - three scenes at Middletoun in the harsh winter of 1937 showing a Great Eastern 'F7' snowbound and surrounded by dogs (not wolves!), part of the gang of labourers numbering 200 who were attempting to clear the line and the horse drawn sledge used by the farmer at Middletoun.   *Mrs D. Hogarth*

It is RECOMMENDED that authority be given for the Passenger train service on the Lauder Light Railway being withdrawn and the Line thereafter worked for Goods and Parcels traffic only.

Authority was duly given and at the end of August 1932 the local newspapers and the *Scotsman* carried an intimation that 'on or after Monday, September 12, passengers will not be conveyed to and from Lauder and Oxton stations on the Fountainhall - Lauder branch railway'. There was little opposition to the move (despite the fact that it meant a cessation of passenger facilities between Lauderdale and the Gala Water) because by then the passenger service had ceased to have any real local significance due to the success of the bus competition. On the evening of Saturday 10th September, 1932 'Maggie Lauder' made her last passenger run, seen off by only a small number of local people. Whether the true worth of the railway had been properly considered is another matter - the following February snow at Soutra Hill resulted in traffic being marooned there all weekend and the *Berwickshire Advertiser* reported that 'Motor bus services between Lauder and Edinburgh are greatly disorganised.' Another cause of discontent was the refusal of the SMT to run a bus replacement for the early train so that for the Heriot's schoolboys and their successors (and indeed anyone with business in the capital before 10 am) daily commuting became an impossibility unless one was prepared to hitch a ride on the fish lorry, or walk, from Lauder over the hill road to Stow.

A recurring feature of these times was the heavy falls of snow which brought chaos to local roads and which blocked the Lauder line on several occasions. In January 1937 blizzards and heavy snowfalls blocked the line near to Middleton and squads of local men, at one time numbering 200, were employed to clear it, each being paid a weekly retainer of 18s. 0d.

Goods traffic continued to be handled, albeit in dwindling quantities, but already the impact of road traffic was being felt upon livestock traffic. Three daily goods trains, hauled by ex-Great Eastern Railway 'F7' class 2-4-2 tank engines and, later, ex-GER 'J67' class 0-6-0 tank engines, were nominally run although they tended to operate 'as required'. The number of staff employed on the line was cut and at Oxton the post of station master was abolished, the last holder of that position being Mr Jim Black. The station was now under the direct control of the Lauder station master, William McConachie, who had replaced Mr Shiel the previous incumbent of that post, but two staff were still employed at Oxton.

By the outbreak of war in 1939 the Lauder line was a somewhat insignificant rural backwater but things were to change dramatically with the opening of a new Ministry of Food 'Buffer Depot' adjacent to Lauder station. This large building was, in effect, a food warehouse and distribution depot of 6,000 tons capacity set up under government control with the aim of providing storage accomodation for staple foodstuffs away from the threat of bombing of the main population centres of south east Scotland. The principal traffic to the depot was flour, which was brought in by rail and distributed by lorry, and to serve the facility a short trailing siding was installed at the western end of the station throat at Lauder.

An 'F7' class and inspection saloon at Oxton on the occasion of the judging of the LNER Scottish Area Best Kept Station Gardens competition, 1932. *Scottish Record Office*

Ex-Great Eastern 'J67' 0-6-0T No. 8492 sent up to work the Lauder line in 1944 and seen here at St Margarets in about 1948. *Authors' Collection*

The basic pattern of goods services were, by now, a Monday, Wednesday and Fridays only mid-morning working from Galashiels and Fountainhall plus a Saturdays only empty van train from Edinburgh to Lauder. This train, hauled by an ex-North Eastern Railway 'J24' class 0-6-0, exchanged its vans for loaded vans at the food depot which were then taken by rail to Leith Docks, to be sent from there as part of the food supplies to Allied troops abroad.

Another important traffic was that of whinstone from Airhouse Quarry - this trade had previously been in the doldrums but the whinstone was now required as hardcore for extending the runways at RAF airfields in the locality. Destinations included Millfield and Charterhall - the latter, situated near Duns, was almost universally known as 'Slaughterhall', it being claimed that the many accidents which occurred during landings and take-offs were caused by the fact that the hardcore had been badly laid on the site by the contractors. On occasions special trains were run for the quarry traffic, both to Fountainhall and beyond and also, from time to time, short workings were run from Hartside siding to Oxton station, where the stone was then loaded onto lorries.

One consequence of war was that female employees appeared on the branch - a notable example being Mrs Mary Fullerton, who was porter-signalman at Oxton for many years before going on to run a guest house in Lauder.

A curious incident occurred on New Year's Day 1941 when a Carlisle-bound freight train had to be divided at Fountainhall into two sections, the main part of the train and a short rear section comprising a wagon carrying bridge girders and the brake van. After the main train had cleared the junction the last two vehicles proceeded to run down at a high speed and took the points for the Lauder branch and, despite the deep snow, they continued up the gradient, smashed through the level crossing gates and came to rest some 400 yards up the line. The guard then emerged from his brake van unhurt but shaken, having been asleep at the time and only awoken by the violent bump caused when the gates were swept away and carried on the front of the leading wagon.*

The immediate post-war days brought fuel shortages and further snowfalls but the spectre of nationalisation now haunted the LNER and, despite a doomed attempt to retain their independence, they were ultimately powerless to prevent the only real attempt then or since to have an integrated transport system in Britain - the Transport Act of 1947.

---

* The accident is recounted in *Main Line to Hawick*, edited by Bill Peacock (Cheviot Publications, 1986).

No. 68511 on a Lauder goods working crossing the Gala Water bridge at Fountainhall, 14th October, 1954.

W.A. Camwell/J.L. Stevenson Collection

The same train between Middletoun and Threeburnford - note the resleepering in progress despite the extremely limited remaining lifespan of the line.

W.A. Camwell/J.L. Stevenson Collection

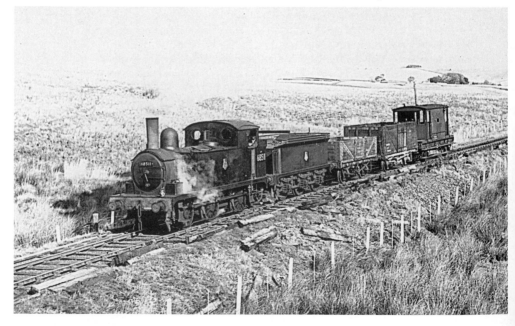

Chapter Five

Grand Finale
FROM NATIONALISATION TO CLOSURE

'But Minstrel Burne can not assuage
His grief while life endureth,
To see the changes of this age
Which fleeting time procureth'
Leader Haughs and Yarrow (Old Ballad)

From 1st January, 1948 the Lauder Light Railway became the property of the Railway Executive of the British Transport Commission or, more popularly, part of British Railways, Scottish Region. However almost before any significant changes could be implemented a catastrophic event ocurred which was to have an effect not only upon the Lauder Light but also on many other railways in the locality including the East Coast main line, the Gifford branch and the Berwickshire Central.

During the early days of August 1948 torrential rain began to fall in Berwickshire and East Lothian and by the 'glorious twelfth' rivers and streams had burst their banks and an immense amount of flooding and damage was being caused. In Lauderdale the full force of nature in torrent was felt but the railway seemed to escape any serious damage. Over the hill, however, this was not so and in addition to minor damage and landslips part of the embankment next to the Gala Water bridge collapsed while the eddy and swirl of the floodwaters scoured and undermined the west abutment and rendered the whole structure unsafe. As the floods subsided the full extent of the damage became apparent. The Commission announced an immediate suspension of all rail services until further notice and emergency road haulage arrangements to and from Galashiels were put in place.

This might well have been the end of the story for the economic case to justify re-opening the line was a very weak one and there were many more pressing concerns for the railway engineers to worry about in that first winter of nationalisation. Time, never the most important factor in the equation when it came to the affairs of this relatively isolated part of the world, went steadily on and the spring arrived but still there was no sign of any action. This prompted the Town Clerk of Lauder to write on 9th March, 1949 to the commercial superintendent of the Scottish Region in the following terms:

> I am instructed to express my Council's grave concern at the prolonged closure of the above line, and to request that arrangements be made with a view to its early re-opening.
> The Council understand that the repairs which would be necessary to enable the railway to function are not extensive.
> I am also asked to draw attention to the very serious situation which would have arisen during the winter had there been a heavy snowfall. As it is stocks of fuel at Lauder station have fallen to practically nil, and the transport available has been taxed almost beyond capacity to supply current needs.

E.R.O. 24533

THE RAILWAY EXECUTIVE
SCOTTISH REGION

R. W. ROSE
District Commercial Superintendent

YOUR REFERENCE

DISTRICT COMMERCIAL
    SUPERINTENDENT.

23 WATERLOO PLACE,

Telephone

OUR REFERENCE

    EDINBURGH.

~~240XIXEXGX~~
CENtral 2477   G.1/28902.
Ext.   275.

18th November, 1950.

A.Y. Henry, Esq.,
Town Clerk,
LAUDER.

Dear Sir,

        With reference to my letter of
the 14th May; I am pleased to inform you
that arrangements have now been made for the
re-opening of the Branch line to Lauder as
from Monday, 20th current, and the
resumption of the normal pre-flood freight
service.

        Yours faithfully,

R.W. ROSE.

This brought the reply that the question of the service to places on the Lauder branch was 'under review but it is not possible at this stage to give any indication as to what the results will be.' A considerable delay then ensued but the damage was eventually repaired and on 18th November, 1950 the Town Clerk received a letter from the Commission stating that 'I am pleased to inform you that arrangements have now been made for the re-opening of the branch line to Lauder as from Monday, 20th current, and the resumption of the normal pre-flood service'. The Town Clerk replied by conveying the Council's 'warmest appreciation' for this. The sole reason for the resumption of the trains was later stated by BR to have been because of the existence of the Food Depot which was still, in the early days of the so-called 'Cold War' seen to have a considerable strategic importance. Had it not been for the Depot it is indeed doubtful if the line would ever have been seriously considered for this re-opening.

The restored service consisted of a single daily trip working, namely one which left Galashiels at 9.26 am and arrived at Lauder at 11.43 am returning from there at 12.15 pm. Subject to a subsequent minor retiming this was destined to be the normal service over the branch until closure. There were now no trains on Saturdays but, for a short time, there was still a Tuesdays - only 'as required' livestock special on the branch which was worked by the locomotive and crew of the Galashiels No. 1 Pilot engine and which connected up with the livestock train from Hawick to Gorgie Market at Edinburgh. Both Hartside and Middleton sidings were still served as required but as from 1st March, 1954 Hartside siding, which had been virtually disused for some time, was closed and Oxton station was reduced to the status of a public unstaffed siding, the station master at Lauder, Mr James Walker, (who, in fact, lived at Oxton) becoming responsible for Lauder, Oxton and Middleton.

The 1950s saw a number of interesting incidents on the line. Perhaps the best remembered was the occasion when George Bell, who ran a bakery and grocery business in Oxton village, was driving his Bedford van over the level crossing at the station there when he was hit by a train. The van was a write-off but Mr Bell escaped with little injury (as the present authors can testify!) and was later aggrieved when BR attempted to charge him for a trespass notice which had been knocked over - the LNER notice, incidentally, has long survived the railway and is still *in situ*. Another level crossing accident occured when an egg-lorry and a train met at Shieldfield and the resulting omelette was an object of great local wonder. An unusual load was carried on the line during this period when a Captain Wade moved his entire farm, including all his stock and machinery, from Trabroun to the South of England by rail. A crane had to be installed at Lauder to handle this traffic and a film was made of this occasion.

New motive power appeared on the branch in the form of brand-new BR Standard 2-6-0 locomotives which were almost certainly the only new engines ever to have worked the line. This move seems to have pre-dated the necessary amendments being made to the original Light Railway Order to permit heavier locomotives to use the line. As a result of an application by BR in June 1955 to the now Ministry of Transport and Civil Aviation, the British Transport Commission (Dornoch and Lauder Branches) Light Railways (Amendment)

The two GER 'J67' tanks which worked the Lauder line from 1944 to 1955 are seen here at Galashiels shed in July 1950, complete with their NBR tenders which carried the water - this unusual form of working was adopted in order to spread weight and comply with the stringent weight limits on the line. Note the two BR liveries. *A.G. Ellis/J.L. Stevenson Collection*

Oxton station looking north, July 1952 - note the LNER trespass notice was knocked down by Mr Bell's van shortly afterwards. *A.G. Ellis Collection*

Lauder branch goods heading for Fountainhall at the Park level crossing, near Oxton, on 26th July, 1952 - apart from the disappearance of the railway little else has changed in 44 years and the scene is still recognisable today.   *C.M. & J.M. Bentley*

Looking towards Oxton from the Park level crossing, 26th July, 1952.   *C.M. & J.M. Bentley*

Branch goods train entering Oxton, 14th October, 1954. Note the broiler on the train and the presence of Mrs Fullerton, the porter-signalwoman.

W.A. Camwell/R.W. Lynn Collection

Lauder from the air on 23rd May, 1952. The branch goods has just left for Oxton while in the foreground is the the large MoD food store complete with private siding and hopper loading system. Behind the station is the main Edinburgh road (the A68) and the town while in the trees lies Thirlestain Castle. The area between the station and the town is now built up.

Crown Copyright/MoD

A view of Lauder station looking west, taken a few moments later.　　*Crown Copyright/MoD*

Lauder station, July 1952. The siding to the food depot can be seen on the extreme right while on the left is the goods shed and site of the engine shed. Note the yard crane and car.

A.G. Ellis Collection

A goods train at Lauder, 14th October, 1954.   *W.A. Camwell/J.L. Stevenson Collection*

Order 1955 was granted, permitting for the first time (officially) an increase in the permitted maximum axle loading from 12 tons to 14 tons. This had been necessitated by the fact that there were now virtually no locomotives still in existence with the former permitted maximum.

This, however, proved to be something of a final development as by the end of the following year rumours were circulating locally that the line was to be closed. This was perhaps not surprising: the absence of any industrial development on the line and the decline of traffic to the Food Depot, coupled with the agricultural revolution begun with the tractor and lorry and ended with the Land Rover and combined harvester effectively meant that the railway had almost completely ceased to have any real part to play in the local economy. In July 1957 the Town Clerk enquired of BR as to whether or not there were any closure proposals and was informed that all branch lines were under periodical review but that no decision to close the Lauder branch had yet been taken. Perhaps a clue to the future was provided for by the fact that an extensive programme of resleepering and refencing had just been carried out between Fountainhall and Oxton; an unfortunate feature on many branch lines at that time being the considerable capital expenditure undertaken when the closure of the line was imminent. A more obvious sign of a run-down was the large numbers of condemned wagons which began to appear in the sidings at Oxton and Lauder. These wagons had become redundant because of a programme of building new purpose-built wagons and a general falling-off of traffic. The depressing sight of these decaying items cluttering up the sidings did little to convince traders that the railway could serve their needs in the modern age.

A review into the viability of the Lauder line was now carried out and in July 1958 a report was submitted to the Transport Users' Consultative Committee for Scotland. The findings of this report were that a total of only 853 tons of freight and 98 head of livestock were being carried over the line annually (the full breakdown of figures is given in Appendix Nine) and that the Ministry of Food Depot, the traffic to which had now been taken over by the Scottish Co-operative Wholesale Society, was now generating no rail traffic whatsoever. All coal was forwarded by road from Galashiels, and all parcels and sundries traffic came from Earlston station by BR lorry and neither of these traffics would be affected by closure. Middleton siding had received one wagon containing 7 tons of fertiliser in the whole of 1957 and it was said that 'the only trader who makes occasional use of this Siding - Mr W.J.D. Elliot, Middleton - has agreed he could not justify its existence.' Alternative facilities, including those for sack hire, would be available and BR could forsee no future developments which would improve the traffic revenue on the branch. The estimated annual savings to the British Transport Commission were £8,597, less an estimated loss of receipts of £1,023 and a nil cost of additional cartage costs, giving an overall net saving of £7,574.

Correspondence now took place between the Lauder Town Council, the TUCC and BR but the only real concern expressed by the Council hinged on the fact that the Food Depot was scheduled to close within the near future, no further deliveries of food being made to it, and that the existence of a railway connection would be very attractive to any future occupier of the site. BR

LMS 2-6-0 No. 46461 on the Lauder goods at Park crossing, 10th July, 1952 - this locomotive did not conform to the limits laid down in the Light Railway Order and its presence on the line was thus unauthorised. *J.L. Stevenson*

Lines of condemned wagons at Lauder, November 1958 - this all too depressing scene was repeated on branch lines throughout the country. *Hamish Stevenson*

A condemned NBR 20T brake van in store at Lauder, November 1958 - a museum piece even then! *J.L. Stevenson*

'V2' 2-6-2 No. 60957 passes Fountainhall with a down freight on 15th November, 1958 - on the Lauder line stand the carriages for the Special. *W.A.C. Smith*

BRITISH TRANSPORT COMMISSION

B.R. 14301/56

S. E. RAYMOND
Chief Commercial Manager
C. J. H. SELFE
Asst. Commercial Manager
Telephone
DOUGLAS 2900
Ext. 213.
Telegraphic Address
COMMERCIAL CENTRAIL
GLASGOW, C.I.
Our Reference B.11.
Your Reference

BRITISH RAILWAYS

CHIEF COMMERCIAL MANAGER
SCOTTISH REGION
87 UNION STREET
GLASGOW, C.I

17th July, 1958.

Andrew Y. Henry, Esq.,
Town Clerk,
Lauder,
Berwickshire.

Dear Sir,

CLOSING OF BRANCH LINES AND STATIONS : LAUDER
FREIGHT BRANCH.

Thank you for your letter of 12th July, and I note that you will write me again after your Council has considered the proposal.

The branch line to Lauder has not been paying its way for some time and it was only the existence of the Ministry of Food Buffer depot which prevented its closure a few years ago. It was made clear to me recently, however, that there was little hope of rail transport being continued for the intake of traffic to the Depot and the information you give me in the third paragraph of your letter confirms a hint I received that the depot would be closed down entirely in the forseeable future.

It is noted that endeavours are being made to attract an industrial user for the premises when they are vacated by the Ministry of Food but, so far, apparently without success. The financial position of British Railways is such that no avenue can be left unexplored in the endeavour to achieve financial parity and the annual saving to be gained by closing the Lauder Freight Branch is £7,574 – quite a substantial sum. In addition to the annual saving involved a considerable sum will be credited to the scheme for the recovery of redundant assets including 10¼ miles of track.

In all these circumstances, therefore, and keeping in mind the usefulness and flexibility of road transport in such rural areas it is felt that it would not be economic to the British Transport Commission to maintain a rail siding to a single industry over 10 miles from its main line connection while British Road Services or British Railways Cartage vehicles are available to provide the transport required by any industry which may take over the vacated premises.

I trust that your Council when considering our proposal will keep these facts in mind and not allow themselves to be influenced unduly by the alleged attractiveness of such a rail siding to any future occupant of the premises.

Yours faithfully,

replied that it would not be economic to maintain a rail siding to a single industry 10 miles from its main line connection and that alternative road services were in any event available. On Tuesday 22nd July a special meeting of the Lauder Town Council was called to discuss the proposed closure of the line and the Town Clerk subsequently informed the TUCC that,

> after the very fullest consideration my Council have decided that in view of the volume of traffic that would appear to be necessary to make the line pay, they cannot make representations against the proposal . . . while naturally regretting it.

Accordingly on Tuesday 30th September, 1958 the last goods train was run over the Lauder Light Railway and as from the following day Lauder and Oxton stations and Middleton siding were closed to all traffic. This was, however, not destined to be the last train for on Saturday 15th November, 1958 Mr Ian Hurst, on behalf of the Branch Line Society, organised what was to be the very last train on the Lauder Light to be used by the public and this train is still remembered with affection in Lauderdale.

All were determined that the passing of the line should be marked in style and at 2.5 pm the special, hauled by a BR Standard 2-6-0 No. 78049 (which was barely three years old at the time) and carrying the Society's black-edged headboard, left Fountainhall witnessed by the enthusiasts, press and BBC television cameras. Two bogie coaches (erroneously said to be the first such vehicles used on the line, notwithstanding the fact that bogie stock was latterly used on the Portobello specials of the 1930s) carried some 155 passengers, each of whom had paid 6s. 0d. to make the journey. The crew of the locomotive were from Galashiels and consisted of Robert Neilson as driver, J. Haig as fireman and H. Romanis as guard. Some of the passengers had special reasons for travelling on this last train and typical of these was James Sharp of Heriot Mill who had as a teenager not only had travelled on the first train (in 1901) but had also been one of the original shareholders in the company, his father having bought him a £10 share as a present. Another was the daughter of the late Revd Allen, historian of Channelkirk parish and an early and enthusiastic supporter of the line.

As the train stormed the hills many local people turned up to pay their last respects and to give 'Maggie Lauder' their own private farewell. At 2.30 pm the train arrived at Oxton where there was to be a 15 minute wait and here passengers clambered off the train to inspect the station where a hundred or more villagers had turned out to mark the occasion and on the final leg to Lauder the lineside was crowded with sightseers at every vantage point. At five minutes past three the train steamed into Lauder where a crowd estimated at 400 or so was waiting. Provost Jolly, the Town Clerk and members of the Town Council (including ex-Provost J. Watson, who was another one to have travelled on the first train) gave the passengers a civic welcome before inviting them to a complimentary tea in the goods shed organised by the Black Bull Hotel and paid for by the Council. While tea was being taken, the engine was fly-shunted to lead on the return journey and a ceremony then took place when an evergreen wreath was placed on the smokebox of the locomotive and Provost

BR Standard 2-6-0 No. 78049 on the very last goods working on the branch at Oxton, 30th
September, 1958.   *J.L. Stevenson Collection*

The Branch Line Society special of 15th November, 1958 prepares to leave Fountainhall with the
last passenger train to Lauder.   *W.A.C. Smith*

Approaching Threeburnford for the last time.   *Hamish Stevenson*

£000   **2nd- HALF DAY EXCURSION**
BRANCH LINE SOCIETY'S RAILTOUR
SPECIAL LAST TRAIN
15th November 1958

Fountainhall   to

LAUDER & BACK
via Light Railway
FARE 6/-   (H)
For conditions see over   £000

Ticket for the Branch Line Society's special on 15th November, 1958.

Provost Jolly attaches the wreath looked on by other councillors and local people.
M.B. Smith

Below: Crowds at Lauder on the final day - more passengers than had been seen for many a long year!
(*Both*) *J. Langford*

After closure - two views of Oxton, 1988 and 1961.   *C. Rubino and G.N. Turnbull*

Oxton station building after closure. *(Both) J. Hay*

Lauder goods shed after closure. *J. Hay*

Jolly then made a short valedictory speech as well as presenting to Mr D. Robertson, a BR delivery driver at Lauder, a Long Service Safe Driving Award.

At 3.40 pm the passengers re-boarded and this time they were joined by members of the Council, travelling in a specially reserved compartment, together with a large number of apparently unauthorised passengers since it was estimated that the total number out of Lauder was in excess of 250! A long blast of the whistle and the final collapse of part of the station platform heralded the departure of the train. To the sound of exploding detonators and cheering crowds the train left the terminus for the last time. At Oxton large crowds were still waiting and a number of the excess passengers alighted. The train then took to the hills for the last time and by the time Middletoun was passed darkness was falling. The train continued on to Galashiels where the passengers then made their own way home and station master Johnston then placed the wreath on the war memorial there. Meanwhile in the cool evening air silence returned to the lineside farms and cottages and the true significance of the event was brought home to all - they had witnessed the end of 'ane auld sang' and there would be no more tomorrows for 'Maggie Lauder'.

A few days later a stores train removed all salvageable items and furniture and gradually the condemned wagons were removed by rail for scrapping and burning, although in a few cases examples were bought locally and ended up as field huts and animal shelters. Several survive to this day on local farms and are mostly of LNER and LMS origin, although there is at least one which still bears the faint legend 'GW' half a century after the demise of the far-away company! The line remained in place for some time before eventually being lifted in the following winter (1960-1) by contractors who used lorries (including an AEC Matador tractor unit) and carried off the rails in short sections. The sleepers (many of which were in a virtually new condition, the line having been re-sleepered shortly before closure) were taken by road to Edinburgh and presumably re-used.

For several years the track remained in place as a shunting spur from Fountainhall Junction to the west side of the Edinburgh Road level crossing, a set of buffer stops being placed next to the gates. The station site at Lauder was taken over by the Council as a roads depot while Oxton station became a private depot. Parts of the trackbed of the line were converted into farm trackways but all bridges were left intact and station buildings themselves survived for many years - those at Oxton surviving until 1993 while the adjacent station master's house, complete with the infamous LNER trespass notice, can still be seen today. The Lauder station site has been redeveloped as an industrial estate and there are few traces left at Oxton but all along the line the remains of level crossings, lineside huts and railway fencing can still be found. It is perhaps unfortunate that the whole trackbed was not utilised as a public road or footpath since the opportunity to create a valuable right of way has thus been lost. But perhaps this is a minor criticism given the background of what subsequently happened to the remaining railways in the locality.

In July 1965 the Berwickshire Central was closed to all traffic, and this included the local railhead at Earlston although the passenger service over this line had not been restored after the 1948 floods. Then the seemingly incredible

Two views of the Edinburgh Road crossing after closure with the remaining section which served as a shunting spur from Fountainhall. *(Both) Gerald Baxter*

Fountainhall station in 1968, some five months before the complete closure of the Waverley Route. *G.N. Turnbull*

Last train at Fountainhall, 6th January, 1969 - 'Deltic' No. D9007 *Pinza* heads the final passenger service (an up special) to Edinburgh while the event is captured for posterity. *Gerald Baxter*

Remains of the day - a girder bridge at Threeburnford and the Airhouse Quarry, June 1994.
A. Hajducki

occurred - to the utter disbelief of Borderers a Labour Government announced its intention to close the entire Waverley route from Carlisle to Edinburgh and, amidst an unprecedented amount of local and and national protest and subsequent recrimination the Waverley route, including the stations at Stow and Fountainhall, closed to all traffic on 6th January, 1969. This was the single greatest line closure ever and prompts questions, even a quarter of a century later, as to how and why a socialist administration so effectively abandoned such a large part of Scotland.* In Lauderdale few had latterly used the trains on the Waverley route after the closure of the branch line but the Waverley closure was a disaster to towns such as Hawick and Galashiels, which had depended on it. A private scheme to re-open the line came to naught but from time to time there are still plans afoot to bring trains back to at least some of the route and at the time of writing (1996) a current scheme to re-open the line between Edinburgh and Hawick is undergoing careful evaluation and costing - this scheme does not, however, envisage the re-opening of a station at Fountainhall. In the meantime the County of Berwick possesses but one railway (part of the East Coast main line) and not a single station while Lauderdale has no railhead nearer than Edinburgh and in the space of a few generations the Railway Age in Berwickshire has both come and gone.

Perhaps the final word on the subject should go to one of the Heriot's scholars who travelled regularly over the Lauder Light so many years ago and who quoted to the authors part of a poem by Ralph Hodgson which he had learnt on his way to school in a third class compartment more than 60 years ago:

'Time you old gipsy man,
Will you not stay,
Put up your caravan,
Just for one day?'

Stow station, 1967. This station served as the railhead for Lauder prior to the opening of the light railway and again, to a lesser extent, after 1933.   *J. Harrold*

* An irony not lost on the local electorate who saw a Labour government implement Beeching cuts which a Conservative administration had not dared to.

Station house, Fountainhall and the Gala Water bridge in June 1994. These two structures are practically the only substantial surviving remnants of the Lauder Light Railway. *A. Hajducki*

Chapter Six

Through the Hills with Maggie Lauder
A JOURNEY ON THE 'AULD LAUDER LICHT'

'Up through the moor to Hartside Farm,
Then by the Quarry round,
And past the Kirk upon the hill,
Right on to Oxton town.'
'The Lauder Light Railway'

The journey to Lauder began at Fountainhall Junction, a small station situated on the mighty Waverley route some 22 miles south of Edinburgh and roughly mid-way between the capital and Newtown St Boswells. The station was a rather sparse affair lying a short distance from the small village of Fountainhall and adjacent to the bridge which carried the road into the village over the Gala Water. The main buildings (including a Nestles chocolate machine remembered with affection by at least one local 'boy') were situated on the down (northbound) platform and a shelter on the up platform and both had been rebuilt when the station had assumed a new importance as a junction. The station was always well-kept and even after becoming unstaffed in its final years the remains of the garden and the decorations carried out to mark the Coronation of 1953 could still be seen. There were two signal boxes at Fountainhall, the old one doing duty as a shed for the level crossing at the north end of the station, while the junction box was constructed new for the opening of the branch line. A substantial station master's house, which survives to the present day, was built in 1870 and there was a small goods yard situated on the up side next to the river.

Signs gave the legend 'Fountainhall Junction Change for Oxton and Lauder', the station having been renamed for the arrival of the branch trains. In the early 1920s a Mr Pringle bombarded the LNER with suggestions that the station and the two or three cottages making up the straggling village should be renamed 'Hoppringle' after a neighbouring hill and farm but the company declined to do so, despite the scholarly but somewhat eccentric pamphlet which accompanied the requests.

Passengers from the south had to cross a footbridge in order to gain the up platform at Fountainhall where there was a bay from which the branch trains left and local folklore still tells of a pompous passenger who was bound for Lauder and who travelled with a large tin trunk. On complaining to the porter after being told that he would have to use the footbridge to cross the line despite his burden and pointing out that he had a tin chest the passenger was promptly told 'Tin chest or brass erse, it's o'er the brig tae Lauder'.

The small branch train normally consisted of two short carriages and a van and, latterly, of a single composite coach and van, and in the lengthy intervals between services the coaches would remain in the bay platform while the engine was despatched to run the goods service and undertake any necessary shunting *en route*.

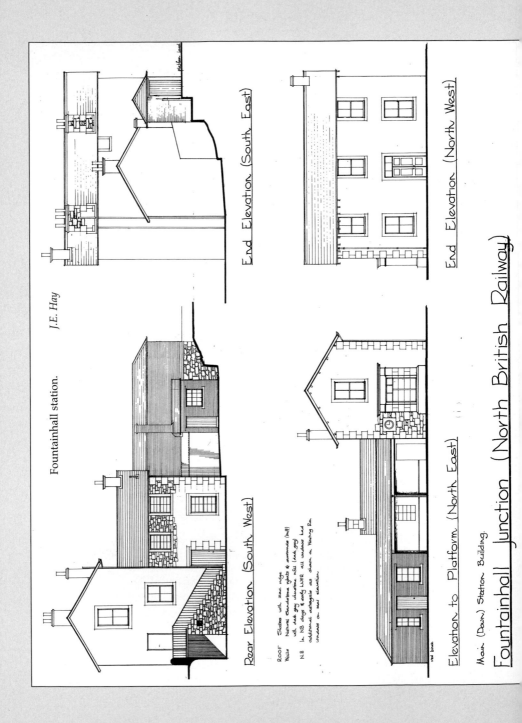

Fountainhall station.

J.E. Hay

End Elevation (South East)

End Elevation (North West)

Rear Elevation (South West)

ROOF   Slates with zinc ridge.
Walls   Natural freestone rybats & surrounds (buff)
         with slate grey vitreous infill (dark grey)

N.B.   In N.B. days & early LNER all windows had
        additional astragals as shown on Rear Ph
        umsheet on rear elevation.

Elevation to Platform (North East)

Main (Down) Station Building.

Fountainhall Junction (North British Railway)

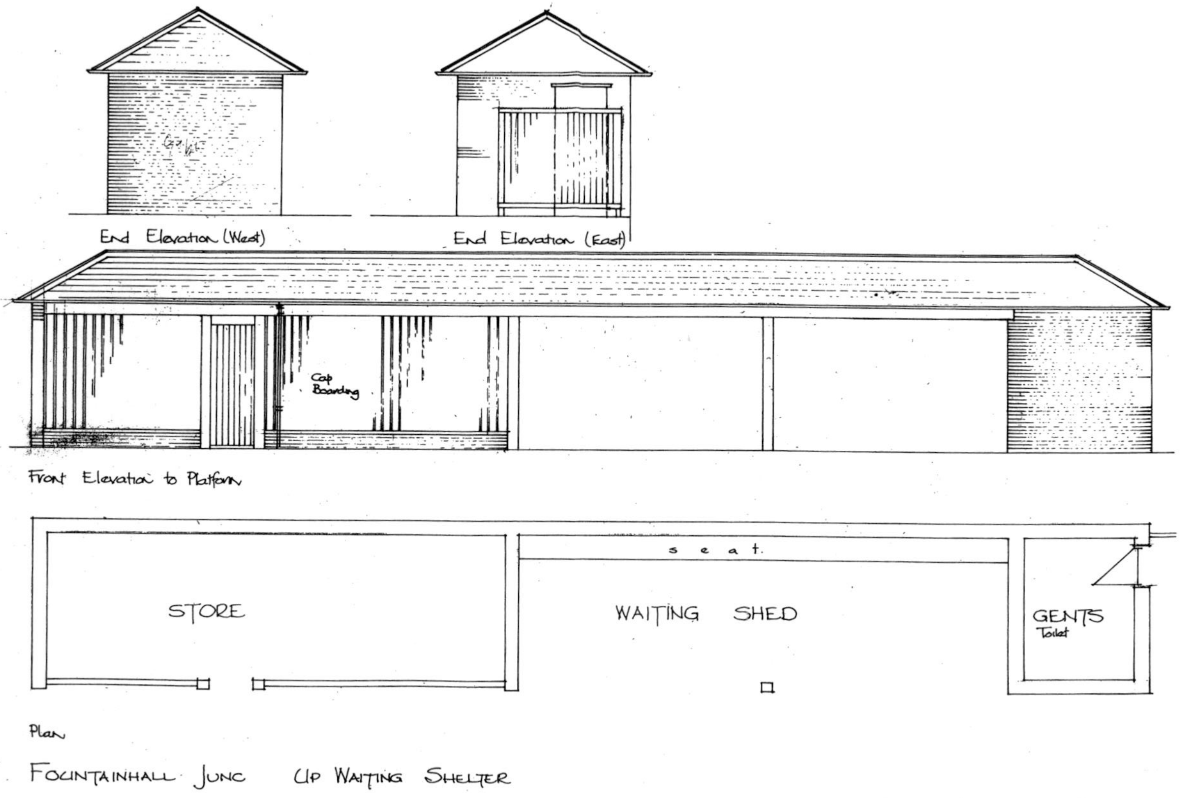

End Elevation (East)

End Elevation (West)

Gap Boarding

Front Elevation to Platform

STORE

seat

WAITING SHED

GENTS
Toilet

Plan

FOUNTAINHALL JUNC UP WAITING SHELTER

J.E. Hay

Fountainhall waiting shelter.

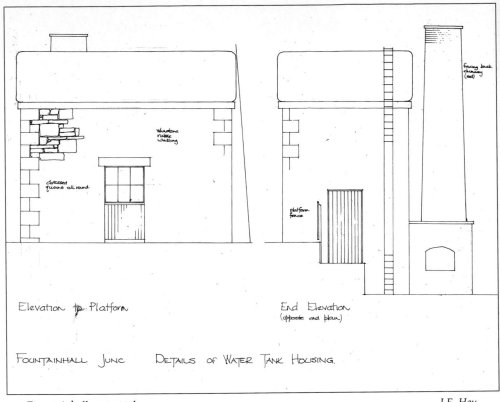

Elevation to Platform

End Elevation
(opposite end plan)

FOUNTAINHALL JUNC   DETAILS OF WATER TANK HOUSING.

Fountainhall watertank.

J.E. Hay

Fountainhall Junction. The two signal boxes are visible - the original one controlling the level crossing and the new (1901) box close to the branch junction.

Reproduced from the 25", 1907 Ordnance Survey Map

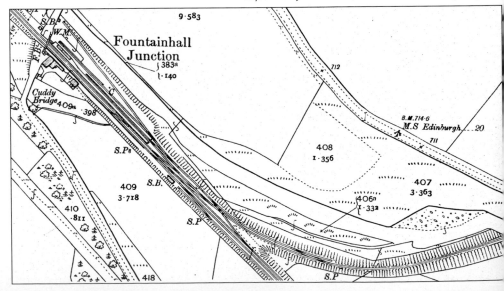

At the appointed time the train would give its customary whistle to the signalman before proceeding southwards for 50 yards or so before swinging to the east away from the main line and heading on a high embankment for a hundred yards to the Gala Water, which the line crossed on a high stone bridge with a single 50-foot arch, the principal engineering feature on the line. Immediately after the bridge came the Edinburgh Road level crossing where the line crossed the main road from Carlisle (the A7) and where the only gates were provided. No crossing keeper was employed here and the trains halted while the crews opened and closed both sets of gates, often causing something of a delay both to passengers and to road traffic. An early proposal to substitute a bridge for the crossing was ruled impracticable on account of the cost and the gradients which would be required and the working of the gates provided an interesting diversion for passengers, particularly children who were often allowed to climb down from the train and assist the guard to close the gates again.

Leaving the crossing the line now turned southwards and followed the main road for a short distance before swinging abruptly north east in a tight arc away from the Gala Water, past Cortleferry and Burnhouse Mains and into the valley of the Nethertown Burn. The line was now beginning a stiff climb at 1 in 50 away from the valley floor and the sound of the little train pounding its way upwards, with the sharp beat of the exhaust and the whistling warning to errant animals was enough to alert the children at Middletoun who would bring their ponies down to a field adjacent to the line and then proceed to race the train. Here a small private siding, for the use of the farm but anglicised by the railway to 'Middleton', was situated on the up side facing Oxton. On occasions the same children, having trained their ponies to jump the cattle guards, would then ride along the line until the whistle of a train behind them would cause them to break into a furious gallop in order to reach the next crossing where they could leave the line.

After Middleton siding the railway continued to climb and close to the watershed and county march between Midlothian and Berwickshire reached the summit of the line at a height of 944 feet above sea level, and some 250 feet or so above that at Fountainhall. The long descent to Oxton began just before Threeburnford, with its two level crossings in the space of a quarter of a mile, and into the narrowing valley of the Mean Burn dominated on the right side by the flanks of the aptly-named Collie Law. The line was by now running almost due north in a very quiet and lonely situation and the only observers of passing trains were the sheep grazing on the steep valley sides and the occasional horse and trap passing on the parallel by-road.

After three-quarters of a mile Hartside siding was reached, again like Middleton a single short siding facing Oxton and on the south side of the line. This facility was a public siding serving the farms of Hartside and Kirktonhill as well as Airhouse Quarry, the latter having a ropeway, small crushing plant and an overhead rail system which carried rock directly from the quarry to the lorry loading facilities and siding. The operation of this system was said to have provided 'great entertainment for little boys' but the quarry finally went out of use in the 1950s after its rock was apparently rejected for use on the Forth Road Bridge project.

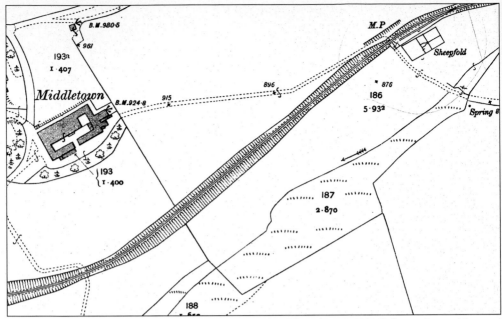

Middletown Siding and Middletoun Farm. *Reproduced from the 25", 1907 Ordnance Survey Map*

Hartside Siding. The parallel courses of the railway, the by-road from Oxton to Threeburnford and the Mean Burn can all be seen, as can Airhouse Wood and Airhouse Quarry.

Reproduced from the 25", 1907 Ordnance Survey Map

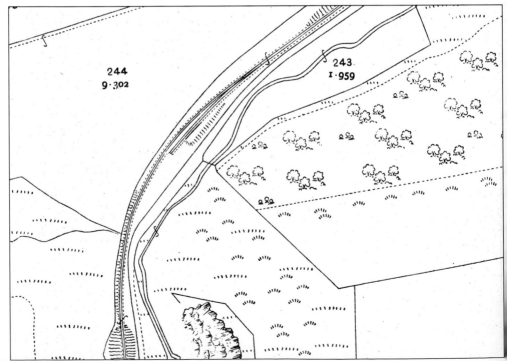

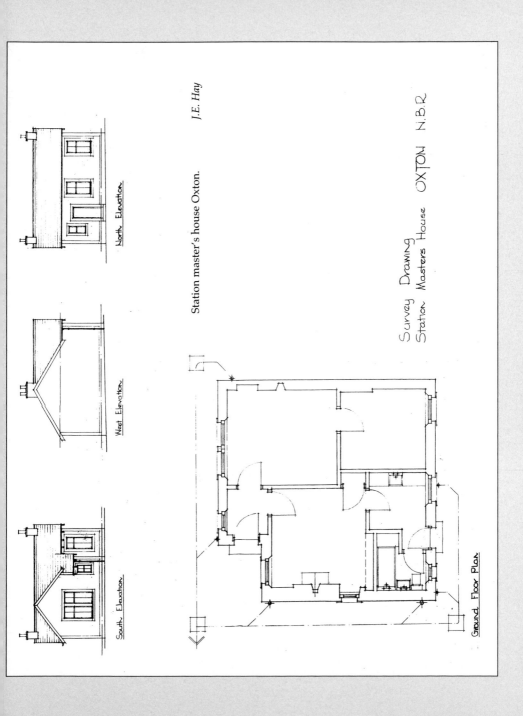

North Elevation

West Elevation

South Elevation

Station master's house Oxton.

J.E. Hay

Survey Drawing
Station Masters House OXTON N.B.R

Ground Floor Plan

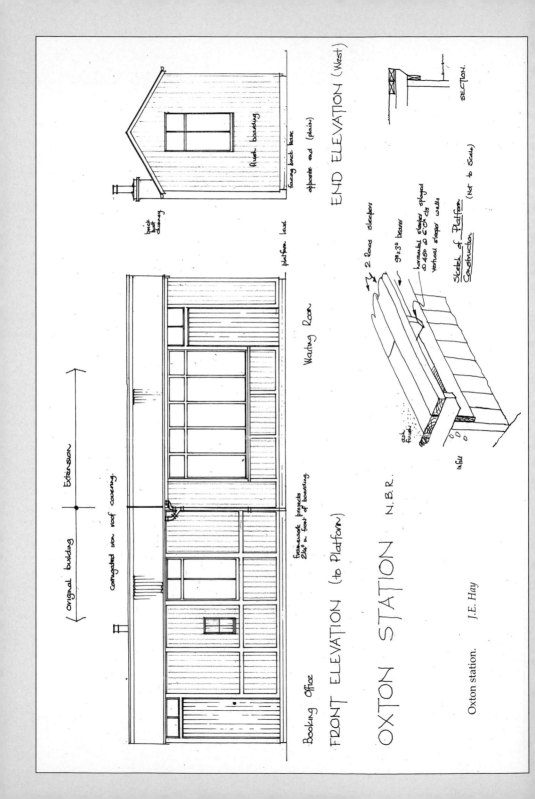

flush boarding

facing brick base

opposite end (plain)

brick built chimney

END ELEVATION (West)

SECTION.

2 rows sleepers

9"×3" bears

horizontal sleeper splayed @ 450 @ 60° ds vertical sleepr walls

Sketch of Platform Construction (Not to Scale)

ash finish

infill

platform level

Waiting Room

Booking Office

original building

Extension

corrugated iron roof covering.

framework projects 2¼" in front of boarding

FRONT ELEVATION (to Platform)

OXTON STATION N.B.R.

Oxton station.   J.E. Hay

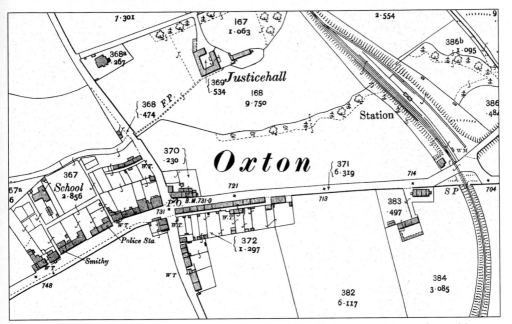

Oxton station and village.

Reproduced from the 25", 1908 Ordnance Survey Map

Lauder station. The Edinburgh to Sedburgh road (A68) runs diagonally through this extract.

Reproduced from the 25", 1908 Ordnance Survey Map

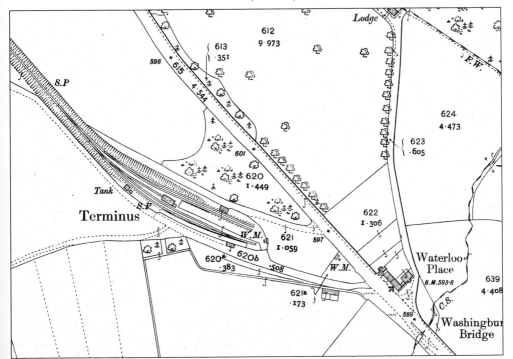

The line now began an immense loop towards Oxton, where it would face southwards and passed close to, but some way below, the ancient site of the parish church at Channelkirk and a Roman fortlet before crossing the road to Oxton at the ungated Park level crossing. Here, as at all other crossings, the engine was required to whistle and this was regarded as something of a dangerous crossing owing to the amount of traffic using the road and the very restricted vision which road users had here.

The line was now running south parallel to the Leader Water and the main A68 road to the east before passing the farm at Justice Hall, named after a former 18th century owner who had entertained an expensive passion for tulips, and entering Oxton station, 6 miles 37 chains from Fountainhall. This station, 'where passengers and gossip are exchanged and the engine pauses for breath', boasted a passing loop, signals, a small platform with station buildings and beautifully kept-up flowerbeds and bushes. The station was on the eastern edge of the village of Oxton and well situated both for passenger traffic and for the collection and uplifting of goods traffic.

Immediately upon leaving the station the main road out of the village was crossed at the point where George Bell's Bedford van came to grief in the 1950s - this was another of the standard pattern of ungated crossing with adjoining wooden cattle grids. The line then swung briefly to the west to avoid a small hillock before resuming its southward downhill run through the dale to Sheildfield and Trabroun, where there were further open level crossings and, on the approach to the latter, a slight uphill climb. From this part of the line the views were more extensive and a wide vista of Lauderdale and of the open sky above could be enjoyed by train passengers. The terminus was now almost in sight before the line dipped slightly to cross the Harry Burn on an impressive single arch stone-built bridge (which still survives) and then turned eastwards once again, passing the site of the later Ministry of Food Depot with its private siding trailing in from the west, before terminating close to the A68 road and on the north-western edge of the Burgh. The station at the terminus consisted of 'an unpretentious wood and galvanised structure' on the single platform, an iron goods shed, a small engine shed, weighbridge and a crane and although the buildings were modest both in terms of design and in respect of the facilities which they provided, the station was perhaps less cramped and more spacious than many typical light railway termini.

From Lauder station a short walk along the main road would bring the tourist to his destination - the impressive Thirlestane Castle, the wide main street of the town or the quiet banks of the Leader and, whichever was chosen, a quiet afternoon could be enjoyed in those golden and almost forgotten times before 'Maggie Lauder' and her clutch of small wooden carriages was ready for the homeward run.

'The Lauder Light Railway'

An original poem rendered at the Lauder Band of Hope Social following upon the opening of the line in 1901 and subsequently reprinted in the local press.

Cheer up, my lads, a mighty change
Has swept across our dale:
The old stage coach has yielded thus
To carriage, steam and rail.

Old order giveth place to new,
The new old ways displace,
And now our good old town
Should wear a brighter face.

For forty years in wilderness
The Israelites did stray,
At length they reached their promised land
Though rough and long their way.

And so for forty years and more
Our railway's been but talk
But now that talk has issued forth
A bright and certain fact.

The puff of 'Billy' in the dale,
The noise of whistle's scream,
Reminds us of an enterprise
Which once was but a dream.

It's not exactly what we hoped
Its pace is rather slow,
It taketh 'Billy' all his time
From Fountain Hall to go.

Up through the moor to Hartside Farm,
Then by the Quarry round,
And past the kirk upon the hill,
Right on to Oxton town.

Of course when nearing Lauder town
It runs a quicker pace -
A tribute this to Royalty
Whose mark is on the place.

And then although its pace is slow
There is some compensation
It giveth time to minds inclined
To serious meditation.

On hills, and fields, and crops and farms
On bird, and flower, and weed
Which surely you'll allow is good
For such as live as speed.

And then there are some other things
Not quite up to our mind,
We'd like a better run of trains
Some lamps our way to find.

Otherwise it is that Light Railway
A harbinger of light,
Should land us down in darkness gross,
And put us in a plight.

We'd like to see two goodly lamps,
Like those at head of town,
Which would ensure our safety
And discourage many a frown.

I pity those poor country folks
Who are on travel bent,
Their doubts, their horrid fears
Their nights so sleepless spent

Less they should miss the early train,
And so their plans destroy;
And I believe, I'm sure I'm right
There ought to be some change.

I hope this ryhme will reach in time
The three director's ears
That at the council round the board
They may dispel our fears;

And grant us better light, and trains
At other times of day.
And we will wish success and speed
To Lauder Light Railway.

D.T.

Appendix Two

Mileages

	Miles	Chains
Fountainhall Junction	0	0
Edinburgh Road L.C.	0	29
Middleton siding	2	11
Threeburnford No. 1 L.C.	3	33
Threeburnford No. 2 L.C.	3	51
Hartside siding	4	53
Path L.C.	5	72
Oxton station	6	37
Sheildfield L.C.	7	77
Trabrown L.C.	9	38
Lauder station	10	33

Appendix Three

A Brief Chronology

30th June, 1898	Lauder Light Railway Order passed and Company incorporated.
3rd June, 1899	Ada, Countess of Lauderdale cuts first sod at Harryburn.
2nd July, 1901	Lauder Light Railway opened to all traffic. Fountainhall station renamed Fountainhall Junction.
1st January, 1923	Lauder Light Railway Company absorbed by London & North Eastern Railway.
12th September, 1932	Passenger service withdrawn, Lauder and Oxton station closed to passengers.
19th September, 1932	Lauder 'signal cabin' abolished and signalling simplified.
1st January, 1941	Accident at Fountainhall.
1st January, 1948	Lauder line becomes part of nationalised British Railways.
12th August, 1948	Line damaged by flooding and service suspended.
20th November, 1950	Line reopened to traffic.
1st March, 1954	Hartside siding closed.
15th June, 1956	Maximum axle load raised to 14 tons.
27th February, 1957	Oxton signal cabin closed, line worked 'One engine in steam'
30th September, 1958	Line closed to all traffic.
15th November, 1958	Last passenger train over branch.
1st April, 1959	Fountainhall Junction renamed Fountainhall.
18th May, 1964	Fountainhall closed to goods.
27th March, 1967	Fountainhall station staff withdrawn.
6th January, 1969	Fountainhall station and whole of Waverley Route closed to all traffic.

Appendix Four

Agreement between the Lauder Light Railway Company and the North British Railway Company, 1899

This Agreement made and entered into between the Lauder Light Railway (hereinafter called 'the Company') - *Of the First Part*; and the North British Railway Company (hereinafter called the 'North British Company') - *Of the Second Part* - Witnesseth, that whereas the Company have been authorised by Order of the Light Railway Commissioners to construct a light railway between Fountainhall Railway Station, in the County of Mid-Lothian (where a junction is effected with the North British Railway system), and Lauder, in the County of Berwick, with all proper works and conveniences connected therewith (hereinafter called 'the Railway': And whereas the North British Company agreed, subject to provisions contained in said Order, to subscribe: to the share capital of the Company up to an amount not exceeding £15,000: And whereas it is provided by Section 13 of said Order that when the North British Railway Company shall have subscribed and paid the sum of £15,000 to the capital of the Company, the Directors of the North British Company may appoint one Director of the Company, who shall be a Director of the North British Company: And whereas it is further provided by Section 38 of said Order that the Company on the one hand, and the North British Company on the other hand, may (subject to the provision of Part III. of the Railways Clauses Act 1863, as amended or varied by the Railway and Canal Traffic Acts 1873 and 1888) from time to time enter into Agreements with reference to, *inter alia*, the construction, maintenance, management, and use or working of the Light Railway: And whereas the North British Company have agreed, on the construction and completion by the Company of the Railway in terms of the said Order, to maintain and work the same: Therefore the parties hereto had covenanted and agreed, and do hereby covenant and agree and bind and oblige themselves, each to the other in manner hereinafter written.

1. The Company shall make, construct, and complete the Railway at, their own expense, in terms of the Order made by the Light Railway Commissioners: and modified and confirmed by the Board of Trade in pursuance of the provisions of Section 10 of the Light Railways Act 1896, and given under the Seal of the Board of Trade, the 30th day of June, 1898, and shall also make, construct, and complete all stations, engine sheds, water columns, and other buildings, works, and conveniences necessary for working the traffic of the railway as a Light Railway, and that to the satisfaction of the Chief Engineer of the North British Company for the time being, and in accordance with plans previously submitted to, and approved of, by the North British Company.

2. When and so soon as the Railway shall have been completed as aforesaid, and approved of by the Government Inspector as ready for public traffic, the North British Company shall take possession thereof, and shall work the whole traffic, local as well as through, of the same, and shall provide the necessary rolling stock and plant for the purpose of effectively working the said traffic, and shall provide at their present station at Fountainhall accommodation for such traffic, and shall maintain the Railway in proper and sufficient condition after the expiry of one year from the date of opening for public traffic.

3. The North British Company shall appoint and pay all Agents, Officers, Booking and other Clerks, servants, porters, and other persons required for maintaining

108

and working the Railway, or required for keeping, in the Offices of the North British Company in Edinburgh, the accounts connected with the traffic, or employed superintending or conducting such traffic, and in maintaining the Railway, and all such officers, clerks, servants, and other persons shall be exclusively under the control of the North British Company, and the Company shall appoint and pay the Secretary and other officers and servants required by them in the management of the capital, finance, and directorial departments of their undertaking.

4. The North British Company shall convey and forward for the Lauder Light Railway all traffic interchanged or passing between the Railway and the North British Railway, and *vice versa*, in the same manner and with the same facilities as if the Railway formed part of the undertaking of the North British Company; and the tolls, rates, and charges, and fares payable for or in respect of said traffic shall, after deduction of the usual clearing house terminals, which shall belong to the Companies respectively entitled thereto, and any portion of through rates or fares which may be due to other parties or companies concurring in such through rates or fares, be divided between the Company and the North British Company, by mileage.

5. The North British Company shall collect and receive in the first instance, all tolls, rates, and charges, and fares due and payable for and in respect of the said traffic, and also of the local traffic of the railway, and the North British Company shall account to the Company for such receipts, and for all incidental receipts such as rent of surplus land, advertisements, houses, grass slopes, &c., and the North British Company shall cause to be kept regular Books of Account of all receipts and payments and other transactions of or in relation to the traffic of the Railway, and shall permit any of the Directors or the Secretary of the Company for the time being, or any other person duly authorised by the Directors of the Company, to have free access to, and to inspect such books of accounts and all other documents relating to the said traffic, at all reasonable times.

6. In respect of the maintenance and working of the undertaking of the Company, and the obligations undertaken by them herein, the North British Company shall be entitled to receive 40 per cent. of the gross revenues of the Company, provided always that if these revenues are less than £10 per mile per week the following increased percentages shall be paid: 45 per cent. if not less than £8 10s. per mile per week, and 50 per cent. if less than £8 10s. per mile per week. All receipts in excess of the sum required to pay a dividend of 4 per cent. per annum on the authorised share capital of the Lauder Light Railway Company shall be divided equally between the Company and the North British Company. The residue of the receipts less the Government duty on the traffic, if accounted for to the Government by the North British Company, shall be paid over by the North British Company to the Company, monthly.

7. The Company shall pay out of their proportion of the gross revenues all feu-duties and all public and parish burdens, including poor rates, school rates, county rates, prison assessments, and other rates and taxes that may be chargeable on the Railway, including the Government duty on the traffic, if not accounted for by the North British Company, and also the expense of the management of the business of the Company, and other charges incurred on their behalf.

8. The Directors of the North British Company shall, by Board Minute, appoint two of their number, and the Directors of the Company shall, in like manner, appoint two of their number not being Directors of the North British Company, who shall together constitute and be a Joint Committee for superintending and developing the traffic of the Company, and for fixing the tolls, rates, and charges, to be levied, or taken in respect thereof. The Boards of said respective Companies having power at any time, by Minute, to change the members representing them in the said Committee, or to fill up any vacancies which may from time to time occur therein. The Chairman of the Joint Committee shall not have a casting vote, and any differences of opinion, when the Committee shall not be unanimous, shall be referred to a standing Arbiter who shall be named by the Committee at the first meeting held by them in each year, and failing such appointment on the application of either of the Companies, by the Board of Trade, and three shall be a quorum of the said Committee.

9. This agreement shall continue and be in force in perpetuity, and the parties bind and oblige themselves to fulfil the whole heads, articles, and provisions of this Agreement each to the other, under the penalty of £1,000 to be paid by the party failing to the party performing, or willing to perform the same over and above performance.

10. All questions, disputes, and differences, which may arise between the parties hereto with respect to the meaning and effect of this Agreement, or of any provisions thereof, or as to the mode of carrying the same into effect other than those otherwise specially hereinbefore provided for, shall from time to time, so often as any such questions or differences shall arise, be referred to arbitration, in terms of the Railway Companies Arbitration Act 1859, and the provisions of that Act with respect to the settlement of disputes by arbitration, shall be held as incorporated with this Agreement and be operative in the same manner as if they were inserted herein.

Lastly. The parties hereto consent to the registration hereof, and of any orders or decreets arbitral to follow hereon for preservation and execution. - In witness thereof, these presents written on this and the two preceding pages by William Bennet M'Cormick, Clerk to Messrs Millar, Robson & M'Lean, W.S., Edinburgh, are executed in duplicate by the parties hereto as follows - viz., They are sealed with the Common Seal of the said North British Railway Company, and subscribed by Alexander Charles Pirie, Merchant, Craibstone House, Auchmill, Aberdeenshire, and John Inglis, Shipbuilder, Glasgow, two of the Directors, and John Cathles, the Secretary of the said North British Railway Company, all at Edinburgh, on the 26th day of May, 1899, before these witnesses, John Martin, Assistant Secretary, and Thomas Henry Short, Clerk in the Head Office, Edinburgh, of said North British Railway Company: And they are executed for and on behalf of the said Lauder Light Railway Company, by Oswald Henderson M'Lean, Secretary *ad interim* of the said Lauder Light Railway Company, at Corstorphine, on the 31st day of said month and year last mentioned, before these witnesses, Norman M'Lean, 1 Mortimer Road, Cambridge, and Arthur Henry M'Lean, W.S., Edinburgh, and are sealed with the common seal of the said Lauder Light Railway Company, and subscribed by the Right Honourable The Earl of Lauderdale, and George Dalziel, W.S., Edinburgh, two of the Directors of the said Lauder Light Railway Company, all at Edinburgh, on the 5th day of June, and year last mentioned, before these witnesses, William White Millar, S.S.C., Edinburgh, and the said Arthur Henry M'Lean.

Appendix Five

Major Pringle's Report

Report made to the Board of Trade by Major J.W. Pringle concerning the Lauder Light Railway

June 31, 1901 [*sic*]

I made an inspection on the 28th of the new works in connection with the Lauder Light Railway.

This railway, constructed under the Order of 1898, commences by a junction with the North British Railway (Hawick branch) at Fountainhall Station in the county of Midlothian, and terminates at Lauder, in the county of Berwick. It deviates laterally at two points beyond the limits shown on the deposited plans, but so far as the Board of Trade is concerned, there is no ground for objection.

The line is single throughout, with passing places at stations and sidings as enumerated below. Land has been purchased for one line only. The gauge is 4 feet 8½ inches, and the space between the double lines is 6 feet. The actual length of the railway is 10 miles 58 chains. The steepest gradient has an incline of 1 in 50, and the longest such gradient extends for a distance of 1 mile 5⅛ furlongs. The sharpest curve has a radius of 9 chains and a length of 23.76 chains. There are no points where reverse curves meet.

The width at formation level is 65 feet. The highest bank and the deepest cutting have a height and depth of 29 and 23 feet respectively. The side slopes in both cases are 1½ to 1.

The permanent way consists of steel flat-bottomed rails weighing 65 lbs. per yard in lengths of 20 feet. Cast iron sole plates are provided on the sleepers next to the rail joints with adjustable clips holding the rail flanges. Each sole plate has two bolts passing through the sleepers. At the intermediate sleepers the rails are fastened by two 5 inch dog spikes.

The sleepers are 9 feet long by 9 inches by 4½ inches in section and area and spaced 2 feet 9 inches apart in the parishes of Stow and Channelkirk, where the speed by the Order is limited to 15 miles an hour. In the parish of Lauder they are spaced 2 feet 6 inches apart where 25 miles per hour is allowed.

The bottom ballast consists of broken whinstone to a stated depth of 9 inches and the top ballast is of ashes.

The ballasting requires to be completed and the sleepers further packed up, and this, I understand, will be done before July 2.

The line before opening will be fenced throughout, chiefly with cross strands of wire 4 feet high.

There has been no difficulty with the drainage.

Level Crossings

There are 30 in all, and of these 11 are public on parish roads and the remainder field or occupation crossings. Of the 11 public roads crossed on the level, only one is provided with gates which close across both the road and the railway. There is no gatekeeper's hut, but the Company is not absolved from maintaining a proper person to open and close the gates. The remaining 10 are provided with cattle grids. Road No. 58 (Channelkirk), referred to in Clause 25(2) of the Order, is one of these, but I understand that the Road Authority have consented to release the Company from the obligation imposed upon them by the Order. No exception was taken by the representative of the Authorities who was present at the inspection to any of the arrangements at these level crossings.

The cattle grids are formed on triangular oak battens, but from the point of view of durability, single iron grids would, I think, be found more sensible.

I have the following requirements to make with regard to the level crossings:

1. The cattle grids require to be examined and spiked down. I noticed some were loose and required fixing.
2. The gates for field and occupation crossings can all be opened inwards towards the railway. Stops should be fixed to prevent this.
3. Some of the posts with notices cautioning users of the public roads to 'Beware of the Trains' require to be fixed in position.
4. Path parish road level crossing. The notice board on the road to the south of the railway should be moved back a further 50 yards, and to the speed posts on the railway in both directions should be added instructions for the driver to whistle.
5. Trabrown parish road level crossing. The notice boards on the road at each side of the railway to be moved back 50 yards from the line.

I observe that the Company have at the request of landowners in some instances provided cattle grids instead of gates for field crossings. I think the Board should make the final decision on the advisability of this action.

Bridging

There are 8 underbridges on the line. Of these 2 are arched having skew spans of 65¾ feet and 15½ feet respectively. The former of these spans the Gala Water. The brick arch has a thickness of 2 feet 9½ inches, and the remainder of the masonry is in whinstone. The bridge has a fine appearance, and as in all other bridges on the line, the masonry is of the highest quality and relects credit on the local masons. The 6 remaining bridges have spans from 6 feet to 15½ feet, and the line is carried in rolled steel beams.

The beams gave a moderate deflection under test load, and have sufficient theoretical strength.

Stations and Junctions

Fountainhall Station

The alterations and signalling requirements in connection with the Light Railway junction at this station are dealt with in my report in R8983. They have been carried out by the North British Railway Company. I have one requirement, viz. that the No. 15 lever should stand locked when Nos. 3 and 2 levers have been pulled.

Oxton Station

At 6 miles 40 chains. There is a loop for pasing trains here and it is a tablet station. There is a siding connection facing down trains, which is locked by the (Fountainhall/Oxton) tablet, and which contains a single lever. There are facing points at each end of the loop. These points are fitted with Annett's serrated bar lock, and have a rod detector on the Home signal. These points are thrown over by a train passing through them in a trailing direction, but these have to be replaced by hand before the Home signal can be pulled off. There is a single lever in each ground frame.

The signals, of which there are 3, *viz.* a Down Home and an Up Distant and Up Home, worked from a ground frame on the platform containing 3 levers, properly interlocked.

I noticed that the facing points at the Fountainhall end were not working properly, and the various points require to be properly connected.

I make the following requirements:

1. That the up platform should be completed and also the fencing at the back before the line is opened for passenger traffic.
2. That the permanent way at the platform ends be gravelled or trunked over also before passenger traffic is worked.
3. That lamps be provided before trains run after dark.

Lauder Station

This is the terminus and a tablet station. There is a single platform line with a larger shelter. There is a run round loop, an engine shed line, and two goods sidings. There is not a turn-table.

There are three sets of points on the passenger line, each of which is controlled by a ground frame with a single lever working Edward's Economical lock and bar. Each ground frame is locked by the (Oxton-Lauder) tablet. A ground frame on the platform containing a single lever working the Down Home signal, which is detected at both sets of facing points.

I might here point out that the ground frame controlling the points at the dead end of the platform is scarcely necessary, and if the Company desire these points and the trap on the siding might be worked by hand with a balance weight lever, and the ground frame removed.

There is no starting signal, and the reference to signals in the Schedule to the Order is possibly misleading. At the terminal station a starting signal is, in the view of the Inspecting Officer, necessary, unless at such a station the Company undertake that there shall never be more than one engine in steam. In this case such an undertaking would not be consistent with the use of Tyer's Tablet, which is the method of working proposed, and I, therefore, make a requirement that the Company should erect a Starting Signal interlocked with the Home Signal. This might possibly be done by converting the single lever which works the 'Home' signal into a 'push and pull' lever.

I attach an undertaking on behalf of the Light Railway that the Electric Train Tablet system shall be the system used on the line for the working of traffic.

Subject to the prior completion of the ballast in and of the requirements noted under paragraphs A, B and C in the foregoing report, and to the provision within two months' time of a Starting signal at Lauder station, I can recommend that the Board grant a certificate to work traffic on the Light Railway under the Electric Train Tablet system with the axle load and at speeds authorised in the Order.

Appendix Six

Locomotives known to have worked the Lauder Light Railway

The following are details of locomotives which are known to have worked on the Lauder Light Railway. Because the line had the lightest axle loading restriction in Scotland (LNER Route Availability 1) these amount to relatively few in number and all were allocated to St Margarets and Galashiels and, at least initially, the branch locomotive at any particular time was kept in the small galvanised iron shed at Lauder.

North British Railway 'R' class 0-6-0T (LNER 'J82')
The first locomotives designed by Dugald Drummond when he became locomotive superintendent of the NBR in 1875. Based on the famous 'Terriers' designed by William Stroudley for the London Brighton & South Coast Railway, they followed LBSCR practice by bearing as names of places served by the company. No. 240 (formerly *Coatbridge* and later *Polton*) worked the first train on the branch but was soon replaced owing to the damage that it and its sister No. 313 (formerly *Clydebank* and latterly *Musselburgh*) was doing to the trackwork. No. 240 survived until December 1924 while No. 313 later became LNER No. 10358 and ended its days as the North Leith shunter (the 'Cundy Pilot') before withdrawal in 1926.

North British Railway 'R' class 4-4-0T (LNER 'D51')
This class had a long association with the Lauder Light Railway. They were also a Drummond design, dating from 1880 and were ideal for branch line work. They were, in the words of Hamilton Ellis, 'extremely neat, and they blended perfectly with the branch lines they were designed to serve. They had small neat wingplates while the solid bogie wheels added to the toy-like appearance of the engines . . . how pleasantly, how gently, the little Drummond tank engine with her brief train loafed up to Lauder'. Although claimed to satisfy the maximum axle loading of 12 tons, they were in fact shown in the official NBR diagrams as having a maximum loading of 12 tons 12 cwt on the leading axle and 12 tons 4 cwt on the trailing driving axles. The initial allocation included No. 33 (the former *Bellgrove*) and then Nos. 103 (LNER 10427) and 98 *Aberfoyle* (10425), the latter probably being the last of its class to work the line. This class operated other local lines such as the North Berwick and Gifford branches and the last ended their days on the Fraserburgh & St Combs Light Railway during the early 1930s.

Great Eastern Railway 'Y64' class 2-4-2T (LNER 'F7')
Designed by Stephen Holden for GER light passenger work in 1909-10, these small locomotives were found to be ideal replacements for the 'D51' class and on the withdrawal of the latter Nos. 8301, 8308 and 8310 were modified to reduce their adhesion and axle weight down to 12 tons and sent to Scotland between September 1931 and October 1932. Nos. 8308 and 8310 were renumbered 7597 and 7598 and worked the Lauder line until their withdrawal in 1944. Because of their large cabs with windows, the 'F7s' were known in London as 'Crystal Palaces' and in Scotland as 'Tomato Houses'.

North Eastern Railway 'P' class 0-6-0 (LNER 'J24')
Designed by Wilson Worsdell for the NER in 1894, several of these light mineral engines were sent to St Margarets to be used on lightly laid lines and members of the class operated the Gifford line and also the Saturdays-only van trains serving the Lauder Food Depot. They were often referred to by the crews as 'Coffee Pots', a rather unfair name for such versatile locomotives.

Great Eastern Railway 'R24' class 0-6-0T (LNER 'J67')

Another GER design, this time from Stephen Holden's father James, this late Victorian class found heavy use on the intensive Liverpool Street suburban services in London. In March 1944 two were sent up to replace the 'F7s', No. 7329 (BR 68492) and, later, No. 7399 (BR 68511). Both were fitted with ex-NBR 'J3'7 tenders and they worked the Lauder branch thus, the idea being that if the water was carried in the tender and not in the locomotive tanks they would comply with the maximum permitted weight due to the weight being distributed over a greater number of axles. They proved an unusual success and lasted until

The last journey - No. 68511 and her tender at Corkerhill, Glasgow on 27th December, 1956, *en route* to Kilmarnock Works for scrapping.   *W.A.C. Smith*

1956.

LMS Ivatt Mogul '2MT' 2-6-0

One of the St Margarets trio of Nos. 46460-46462 was known to have worked the branch for a short period in 1952, despite the fact that it did not comply with the weight restrictions. The reason for this is not known.

BR Standard '2MT' 2-6-0

The final class of steam locomotive to work the line, these were built at Derby Works from 1953 onwards to a modified LMS design and had a maximum axle weight of 15 tons. After the imposition of a higher weight restriction, they were permitted to work the line officially and a member of the class, No. 78049, worked the final passenger service over the branch in 1958.

English Electric 350HP 0-6-0 diesel shunter (class '08')

One of these locomotives was seen on the line on several occasions in 1958 and on at least one of these occasions appeared to be heading the normal return trip working over the branch. With a tractive effort of 35,000 lb., the English Electric shunters were the most powerful ever to travel over the Lauder line!

Last train at Oxton - note the platelayer's trolley shed and the remains of the once-fine station garden. *J.L. Stevenson*

Preparing for the last working from Lauder - No. 78049 backs her coaches out towards Harryburn bridge. *Hamish Stevenson*

Appendix Seven

Last Train on the La'der Licht

This lively eye-witness account of the line's last day was written by Michael B. Smith when a pupil of Dundee High School and was published in the school magazine in December 1958. The authors wish to thank both Mr Smith and Robert Nimmo, the present-day Rector of the school, for their permission to reprint it here.

On the morning of Saturday 15th November, 1958, rather more than the usual flow of passengers were seen to be converging on No. 3 platform at Edinburgh (Waverley) to join the 12.52 pm for Gorebridge and Hawick. Some people were taking it as usual back to Dalkeith or Hawick, but for many it was a memorable occasion, but a melancholy one. For it was the last time a train was to run to Lauder on the little railway from Fountainhall.

There were many visitors from a distance, but some of those who were taking the train had known the line for years; some were bringing their children to show them how things had been. It felt like a family occasion, so that complete strangers spoke to each other and were gathered into the community for the trip.

Seven coaches were provided and were loaded to capacity. The run was made over former NB metals to Fountainhall which was as far as most people were going. From Waverley, it runs through some rather regrettable Edinburgh outskirts and down into more placid scenery, dotted with slag heaps and mining towns, notably Newtongrange, and finally, into bleak, rugged country - the country of the great hills.

Most of the stations have been modernised with new name-boards, etc., but a few antique survivals, like iron drinking fountains with the admonitory words, 'North British Railway. Keep platform dry,' still survive, pointing to an older, more rugged age in railway work.

As the train drew into Fountainhall, the platform positively groaned with its unaccustomed weight of passengers, waiting for the special train which was to take us to Lauder. This normally quiet little place must have done its biggest business in years!

As we waited for the 'Special' to back into the bay platform, there was time to think of the events that brought about the railway.

In the 'nineties, Lauder's only connection with the outside world was a road carriage from Stow station. After an 1896 Act, an opportunity was taken to build a line from Lauder to Fountainhall. The first sod was cut in June, 1899, by Lady Lauderdale, and in 1901 the line, some 10½ miles long, was brought into operation, amidst great public rejoicing.

During its independent existence, it proved financially successful and passed to the LNER in 1923.

But, as with so many branches, the advent of the bus brought about a decline in traffic and on 10th September, 1932, the last passenger train ran. The goods traffic left came from a Ministry of Food depot at Lauder but, when it closed in October, it brought about the complete closure of the line. Very soon the rails will be lifted.

And now, back to the train. After everyone had found a seat in the two coaches (and there were about 130 people), with a whistle it jerked away and veered left over a magnificent viaduct, over the Gala Water to a level crossing. This bridge was damaged in the floods of 1948 and, as a result, the line was closed from 1948-1950.

The guard operated the gates of the crossing, and soon we were on our way. The line soon swung NE to start its climb over the Lammermuirs. The line abounds in sharp curves and gradients. On each side of us the bleak, cold hills, enshrouded in mist, looked down on us with what seemed like a metaphorical tear in their eyes.

The little engine was soon climbing hard, but a little later the summit was reached and

The guard attends to the Edinburgh Road crossing gates for the penultimate time as locals look on at the passing of an era.

J.L. Stevenson

Est. 33—200,000—3/38 ⊹

LONDON & NORTH EASTERN RAILWAY

B 852

COMPARTMENT RESERVED

3.40 Am ___ **Train** ___ **Date** 15ᵗʰ *Novʳ* 19*58*

Name LAUDER TOWN COUNCIL

From LAUDER

To FOUNTAINHALL

Signature

we were coasting down into Oxton, the only intermediate station on the line. It was an unpretentious wood and galvanised iron structure, strangely enough, recently painted. Unfortunately, the platform has been knocked away so that there was quite a jump to get on to it.

Oxton station was notable for its fine, flowering shrubs, the remains of a station garden. But, partly due to the oncoming winter and partly to the many enthusiasts' feet, they were not perhaps at their best! The whole population of Oxton was there to see the little train. The remains of the platform slid still farther to the ground under the many people rushing about there. Many photographs were taken there, and soon when everyone, including a band of loyal locals, had rejoined the train, it moved off, surrounded by people.

The little train fairly raced down the bank towards Lauder and as it slowed up round the bend to Lauder, passing some condemned wagons, left to lie there in obscurity till the demolition train came, we could see the tremendous crowd gathered on the platform. They numbered some 800 people. Again, out came the cameras, this time including some newspaper and television cameras.

After a minute or two, the Provost made a speech on the 'death' of the little line and then presented the driver of the BR lorry, which was to take over the freight, with a safe driving medal. He then solemnly placed a wreath on the engine. Again this was recorded on film.

Tea, provided by the inhabitants of Lauder, was then served in the nearby goods shed. The station buildings here, too, had been freshly painted and the platform was still intact and littered with dead leaves.

About half an hour later, after the engine had managed to round its train, crushing many pennies in its path, we were ready to move off, being joined by the Provost and the Council.

Amidst the noise of many detonators and crammed with still *more* locals, we set off down the track. In our compartment was a man who had been on the first train, 57 years ago. He told us what it was like and showed us some tickets which he had bought when the line was still open.

At Oxton, we dropped a crowd of local people and soon after, we were on our way again, back over the Lammermuirs, over many crossings protected by cattle grids. It was growing dusk as we attempted the level crossing, where the guard got out and opened the gates. Over the Gala Water we went, and into Fountainhall.

Studying the name-board, 'Fountainhall Jcn.' we wondered what people would think in future seeing the 'Jcn.' part and wondering where on earth the junction was.

Night fell. It was to be the last night, as far as the little railway was concerned, for very soon, the only witnesses left as to its path would be the stations, the crossings and the silent grey viaduct which faded away as we watched, nostalgically, into the dark of night.

<u>Lauder Light Railway</u>

<u>Special Last Train</u>

15th November 1958

<u>T E A   T I C K E T</u>

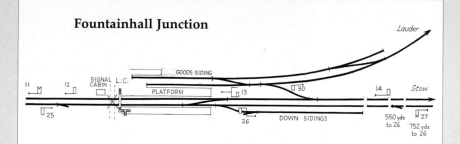

Fountainhall Junction

Lauder

GOODS SIDING

11   12   SIGNAL L.C.
CABIN   PLATFORM   13   30   14   Stow
25   26   DOWN SIDINGS   550 yds   27
to 26   752 yds
to 26

OXTON SIGNALLING DIAGRAM 1955

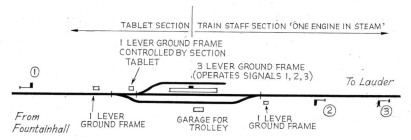

TABLET SECTION | TRAIN STAFF SECTION 'ONE ENGINE IN STEAM'

1 LEVER GROUND FRAME
CONTROLLED BY SECTION
TABLET

3 LEVER GROUND FRAME
(OPERATES SIGNALS 1, 2, 3)

① To Lauder

From
Fountainhall

1 LEVER
GROUND FRAME

GARAGE FOR
TROLLEY

1 LEVER
GROUND FRAME

②   ③

LAUDER SIGNALLING DIAGRAM 1930

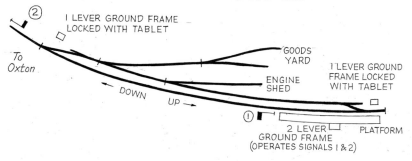

②   1 LEVER GROUND FRAME
LOCKED WITH TABLET

To
Oxton

GOODS
YARD

1 LEVER GROUND
FRAME LOCKED
WITH TABLET

DOWN   UP

ENGINE
SHED

①   PLATFORM

2 LEVER
GROUND FRAME
(OPERATES SIGNALS 1 & 2)

LAUDER 1950s

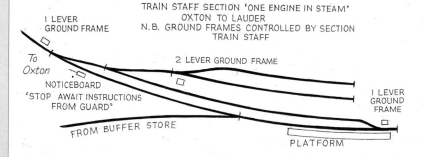

TRAIN STAFF SECTION 'ONE ENGINE IN STEAM'
OXTON TO LAUDER
N.B. GROUND FRAMES CONTROLLED BY SECTION
TRAIN STAFF

1 LEVER
GROUND FRAME

2 LEVER GROUND FRAME

To
Oxton

NOTICEBOARD
'STOP AWAIT INSTRUCTIONS
FROM GUARD'

1 LEVER
GROUND
FRAME

FROM BUFFER STORE

PLATFORM

Appendix Eight

Signalling on the Lauder Light Railway

The line was operated by means of the electric tablet system and the particular one in use on the branch was the Tyer's No. 6 tablet. The signalling contractor for the works was the Railway Signalling Company Ltd, of Fazakerley, Liverpool. The line had lower quadrant signals throughout its life and the system was basic but to passenger standards until at least 1932. The line was divided into two sections, namely (i) Fountainhall Junction to Oxton and (ii) Oxton to Lauder. Technically there was a block post at both Oxton and Lauder but in both cases there was little more than basic semaphore signals and points operated from a ground frame on the platform. The electrical tablet instruments were housed in the station office at both places and were operated by a porter-signalman (or signalwoman in the case of Oxton!)

The Lauder 'signal box' was closed on 19th September 1932, seven days after the passenger service was withdrawn and signalling alterations were then put into effect. The section from Fountainhall to Oxton continued to be worked by No. 6 tablet, but from there to Lauder the line was worked as 'one engine in steam'. A train staff lettered 'Oxton and Lauder', with Annett's key attached, was provided and kept by the train staff custodian at Oxton. At Lauder the ground frame located on the station platform and the signals operated therefrom were dispensed with. A new single lever ground frame, released by Annett's key, was provided at the point leading to the goods yard and a similar installation was provided at the platform loop points. The two other existing single lever frames - tablet worked - at Lauder, were removed, as were the tablet instruments for the Oxton - Lauder section. Oxton remained in operation as a 'signal box' until 27th February, 1957 and thereafter the whole branch was operated as 'one engine in steam'.

At Fountainhall Junction the original signal box at the level crossing was reduced to a gate box on 30th June, 1901 when a new signal box was provided at the junction with the Lauder branch. This new box was replaced by a new brick structure opened on 2nd May, 1954 and this outlived the Lauder branch, being finally closed with the rest of the Waverley line on 6th January, 1969. Its lever frame, together with a 'totem' nameboard from Fountainhall station is now preserved at the Royal Museum of Scotland in Edinburgh.

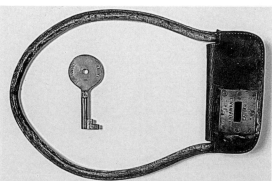

The branch token and token pouch (both suitably inscribed) used in the final years of the branch.   *M.B. Smith and Rae Montgomery*

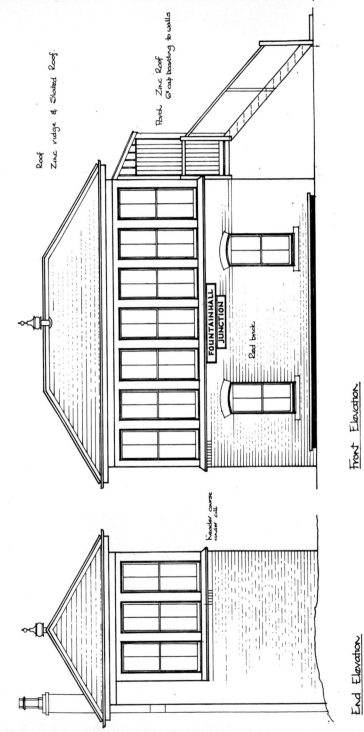

Roof
Zinc ridge & Slated Roof.

Porch Zinc Roof
& cab boarding to walls

FOUNTAINHALL
JUNCTION

Red brick

Header course under cill

End Elevation

Front Elevation

FOUNTAINHALL SIGNAL BOX N.B.R.

The signal box at Fountainhall, opened in 1901 and replaced with a more modern structure in 1954. *J.E. Hay*

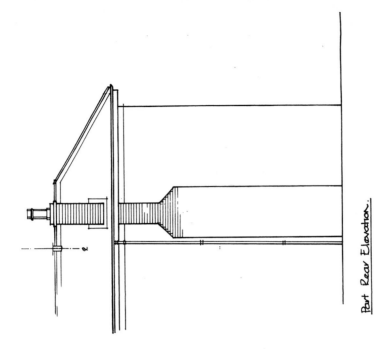

Part Rear Elevation.

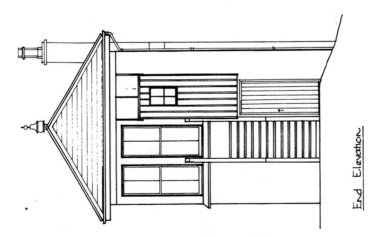

End Elevation

Appendix Nine

Traffic Statistics

(a) Statistics 1901-1934

LAUDER

Year Ending	PASSENGERS		FREIGHT			
	No.	Receipts	Goods	Sheep	Livestock	Receipts
	£	£	tons	head	(other)	£
31. 01. 1902	7,769	693	4,558	1,539	429	320
31. 01. 1903	9,564	1,002	7,591	3,720	401	669
31. 01. 1904	8,797	1,004	7,449	3,487	320	641
31. 01. 1905	9,114	1,013	7,482	3,074	316	625
31. 01. 1906	9,513	1,042	7,862	3,567	414	627
31. 01. 1907	9,052	989	7,353	4,986	423	618
31. 01. 1908	9,305	1,035	8,159	4,279	338	668
31. 01. 1909	8,557	1,025	7,706	3,862	299	612
31. 01. 1910	7,990	958	7,331	4,676	368	562
31. 01. 1911	7,617	996	7,567	3,773	479	582
31. 01. 1912	8,236	1,035	8,539	5,106	330	643
31. 12. 1912 (a)	6,646	884	6,751	4,287	229	623
31. 12. 1913	7,949	1,063	7,983	3,965	411	564
31. 12. 1914	7,388	996	5,176	4,296	597	483
31. 12. 1915	6,679	938	8,070	5,424	534	485
31. 12. 1916	5,319	850	6,920	6,701	603	454
31. 12. 1917	4,582	827	5,134	6,718	634	494
31. 12. 1918	4,502	812	8,181	5,619	540	678
31. 12. 1919	8,166	1,734	9,005	7,995	547	970
31. 12. 1920	7,887	1,808	10,061	7,951	723	1,436
31. 12. 1921	6,258	1,729	16,005	8,965	652	1,358
31. 12. 1922	7,196	1,620	10,559	11,007	912	1,121
31. 12. 1923	7,614	1,529	13,743	10,487	1,022	623
31. 12. 1924	6,141	1,218	18,768	8,643	1,356	717
31. 12. 1925	5,735	1,128	16,196	6,667	1,373	439
31. 12. 1926	4,177	900	14,823	6,774	711	437
31. 12. 1927	3,542	752	11,277	6,128	1,059	432
31. 12. 1928	2,377	557	6,095	7,426	1,120	502
31. 12. 1929	2,322	531	7,675	4,805	708	294
31. 12. 1930	1,927	405	4,339	5,282	829	355
31. 12. 1931	1,437	318	19,099(b)	9,586(b)	n/a	1,104
31. 12. 1932	939	126	5,625(b)	8,006(b)	n/a	739
31. 12. 1933	225(c)	94(c)	4,383(b)	n/a	n/a	462
31. 12. 1934	159(c)	40(c)	3,610	n/a	n/a	327

OXTON (including Hartside and Middleton)

Year Ending	PASSENGERS		FREIGHT			
	No. £	Receipts £	Goods tons	Sheep head	Livestock (other)	Receipts £
31. 01. 1902	6,037	319	2,661	4,739	130	157
31. 01. 1903	7,975	435	3,871	9,730	492	269
31. 01. 1904	7,976	447	4,281	10,109	565	283
31. 01. 1905	7,626	451	4,151	12,436	511	257
31. 01. 1906	7,110	440	4,313	11,501	604	265
31. 01. 1907	7,547	460	4,733	12,374	511	257
31. 01. 1908	7,210	450	3,670	12,636	486	246
31. 01. 1909	6,209	415	4,115	13,396	596	257
31. 01. 1910	5,827	430	4,043	13,901	550	286
31. 01. 1911	5,617	418	3,822	14,118	591	245
31. 01. 1912	5,312	386	5,312	13,805	448	241
31. 12. 1912 (a)	4,510	320	3,184	11,415	405	189
31. 12. 1913	5,987	426	3,993	14,156	526	244
31. 12. 1914	5,779	418	4,437	17,630	745	299
31. 12. 1915	5,625	428	4,205	15,231	687	279
31. 12. 1916	4,117	456	3,187	15,458	718	224
31. 12. 1917	3,325	413	3,565	16,252	732	351
31. 12. 1918	4,081	482	3,592	15,660	712	421
31. 12. 1919	5,242	649	3,871	14,668	685	542
31. 12. 1920	5,670	755	3,314	14,864	538	832
31. 12. 1921	4,862	758	5,614	15,801	504	994
31. 12. 1922	5,136	789	5,041	17,198	389	620
31. 12. 1923	5,442	824	16,572	16,902	527	1,265
31. 12. 1924	5,515	671	17,273	18,444	775	1,632
31. 12. 1925	4,830	564	15,336	14,513	931	1,681
31. 12. 1926	4,128	508	13,825	14,227	640	1,552
31. 12. 1927	3,142	418	10,845	9,864	763	1,106
31. 12. 1928	2,239	337	5,756	10,153	640	1,552
31. 12. 1929	2,136	231	6,902	8,245	574	770
31. 12. 1930	1,768	221	4,207	6,973	772	648
31. 12. 1931	1,193	126			(d)	
31. 12. 1932	932	85			(d)	

Notes:
(a) Period 1.2.1912 to 31.12.1912 only;
(b) Figures include Oxton, Middleton and Hartside;
(c) Excursion traffic;
(d) Figures included with Lauder.

(b) Statistics from BR Report of July 1958

Traffic dealt with 12 months ended 31st December, 1957

Since the handling of traffic into and out of the Ministry of Food Buffer Depot was taken over by the Scottish Co-operative Wholesale Society Ltd, the principal traffic now dealt with on the branch is relatively small quantities of agricultural traffic mainly potatoes and fertilisers.

Passenger Rated Traffic

	Lauder	
	Trucks	*Heads*
Livestock Direct Load	1	1

Freight Rated Traffic
Forwarded Full Truck Loads

	Middleton Siding		Oxton		M.O.F. Depot		Lauder		Total	
	Wagons	*Tons*	*Wagons*	*Tons*	*Wagons*	*Tons*	*Wagons*	*Tons*	*Wagons*	*Tons*
Goods	-	-	6	43	-	-	30	262	36	305*
Minerals	-	-	-	-	-	-	-	-	-	-
Coal class	-	-	-	-	-	-	-	-	-	-
Livestock (head)	-	-	2	28	-	-	-	-	2	28
Forwarded	-	-	8	43	-	-	30	262	38	305
Total			Head	28					Head	28

Received Full truck Loads

Goods	1	7	1	6	-	-	25	87	27	100
Minerals	-	-	14	132	-	-	32	310	46	442
Coal Class	-	-	-	-	-	-	1	6	1	6
Livestock (head)	-	-	1	14	-	-	4	56	5	70
	1	7	16	138	-	-	62	403	79	548
			Head	14			Head	56	Head	70
Total Forwarded	1	7	24	181	-	-	92	665	117	853
and Received			Head	42			Head	56	Head	98

* This includes 272 tons of 'glut' potatoes which is of a non-recurring nature.

In addition to the full load traffic conveyed over the Lauder Branch the following parcels and sundry goods traffic for Lauder and Oxton was dealt with at Earlston and collected and delivered in these places by British Railways motor vehicles:

Passenger rated traffic		*Freigth rated traffic*	
Forwarded	*Total No.*	*Forwarded*	*Total tons*
Parcels Recieved	84	Sundries to Earlston by motor	11
Parcels delivered to consignees			
by Earlston motor	2,136	*Received*	
Parcels addressed TCF ('to be		Sundries from Earlston by motor	104
called for') left at Lauder by motor	42	Sundries TCF Lauder	7
	2,262		122

Sources, Acknowledgements and Bibliography

So far as the authors are aware, this is the first book that has ever been written on this somewhat esoteric subject and they have gathered information from a wide range of sources. These include that invaluable repository, the Scottish Record Office, which remains the principal source for any Scottish line history. In addition valuable information was gained from the records of and the staff and officials of National Monuments Register of the Royal Commission on the Ancient and Historical Monuments of Scotland, the National Library of Scotland, the Scottish collection at the Edinburgh Central Public Library, the University of Glasgow Archives, the Mitchell Library, Glasgow, the Glasgow Museum of Transport, the Ministry of Defence, the Thirlestane castle trustees, the *Southern Reporter* newspaper, the University of Aberdeen, the Public Record Office at Kew and the National Railway Museum, York. Thanks is given to those of the above bodies who generously consented to the reproduction here of materials within their possession. In addition the local newspapers of the day (an often ignored source of railway history) provided much information and entertainment.

A large number of individuals gave generous help and encouragement and these included past and present inhabitants of Lauderdale who helped to give the book some of its more human interest. The authors would like to mention in particular Gerald M. Baxter, J.M. Bentley, J. Britton, Alan W. Brotchie, William Boyd, R.M. Casserley, Godfrey R. Croughton, Bruce Ellis, David Harvey, Jim Hay, Andrew Henry, Mrs Dot Hogarth, Jeff Hurst, Peter Jarvis, John Langford, Sandy McLean, Bill Lynn, John Minnis, Ian W. Mitchell, Ed Nicoll, Jim Page, Bill Rear, Dr R.A. Read, Bill Sewell, Marshall Shaw, Mike Smith, W.A.C. Smith, Hamish Stevenson, Ian Stevenson, J.L. Stevenson, Norman Turnbull, Francis Voisey, Bill Walker, J.S. Webster and Peter Westwater. Thanks are also due to Anne Whitfield, for typing out the MS, and to our ever-patient publishers. Lastly two useful addresses are that of Bill Lynn, the Membership Secretary and Treasurer of the North British Railway Study Group at 2 Brecken Court, Saltwell Road South, Low Fell, Gateshead, NE9 6EY and Mr Ian W. Mitchell of R. Clapperton, The Studio, 28 Scotts Place, Selkirk, TD7 4DR from whom copies of the charming early prints of the line featured in the book can be obtained.

Further information about a variety of matters can be found in the following brief bibliography of secondary sources:

Local history and topography

The New Statistical Account of Scotland - II. Berwickshire, 1845
Ordnance Gazetteer of Scotland, 1895
The Third Statistical Account of Scotland - Berwickshire, 1990
The History of Channelkirk Parish, Allen, 1902
Lauder and Lauderdale, Thomson, 1902
Tweed Tributaries - Gala, Leader and Leithen, Eckford, 1945
Lauder - a Free Burgh for Ever, Scott, 1992

Railways and transport:

The North British Railway, Hamilton Ellis, 1955
The North British Railway, Thomas (2 vols., 1969,1975)
Locomotives of the NBR 1846-1882, SLS, 1970
Locomotives of the LNER, RCTS (various dates)
From SMT to Eastern Scottish, Hunter, 1985
'The Lauder Light Railway', Hamilton Ellis, *Railway Magazine*, January 1930
'Last Train to Lauder', *Branch Line News*, December 1958
'On the track of the Lauder Light', Mackay, *Scots Magazine*, October 1970
'The Lauder Light Railway', Hay, *NBRSG Magazine*, 1976
'The Lauder Light Railway', Reid, *NBRSG Journal*, 1987

Index